Three
Medieval
Views of
Women

Three Medieval Views of Women

La Contenance des Fames
Le Bien des Fames
Le Blasme des Fames

Translated and edited by
Gloria K. Fiero
Wendy Pfeffer
Mathé Allain

Yale University Press
New Haven and London

Published with assistance from the foundation established in memory of Philip Hamilton McMillan of the Class of 1894, Yale College.

Designed by Jo Aerne and set in Sabon type by The Composing Room of Michigan.
Printed in the United States of America by Thomson-Shore, Dexter, Michigan.

Library of Congress Cataloging-in-Publication Data
Three medieval views of women : La Contenance des fames, Le Bien des fames, Le Blasme des fames / translated and edited by Gloria K. Fiero, Wendy Pfeffer, Mathé Allain.
          p.   cm.
     Bibliography: p.
     Includes index.
     ISBN 0–300–04441–0 (cloth); 0–300–04442–9 (pbk.)
     1. French poetry—To 1500—Translations into English.   2. Women—History—Middle Ages, 500–1500—Sources.   3. Women—Poetry.   4. English poetry—Translations from French.   5. French poetry—To 1500.   I. Fiero, Gloria K.   II. Pfeffer, Wendy, 1951–
III. Allain, Mathé.   IV. Contenance des fames.   1989.
V. Bien des fames.   1989.   VI. Blasme des fames.   1989.
PQ1327.D5T47   1989
841'.1'0809287—dc19   88–37431
                              # 18780652   CIP

The paper in this book meets the guidelines for permanence and durability of the Committee on Production Guidelines for Book Longevity of the Council on Library Resources.

10 9 8 7 6 5 4 3 2 1

Contents

Illustrations

Preface

The three poems that form the subject of this study represent a relatively unexplored medieval genre, the *dit* (from the French *dire* = "to say," hence "something said"). *Dits* differ considerably from other vernacular literary forms. They lack the grandeur and breadth of the medieval epics, the lyrical grace and passion of the troubadour songs, the narrative zest of the best *fabliaux,* and the spiritual depth of medieval religious verse. Nevertheless, the three *dits* presented here are among the freshest, most engaging examples of medieval literary expression. Written down in the late thirteenth and early fourteenth centuries, these Old French poems bear some kinship to the lyrics of the troubadours and trouvères, poets whose concerns with worldly matters—romantic love and martial deeds, among others—provide insight into medieval secular life. Structurally the *dit* resembles the *fabliau,* a humorous tale in general without serious intent but occasionally carrying a moral. Unlike the *fabliau,* the *dit* is expositional rather than narrative and usually develops an idea or theme. In the case of the three *dits* that constitute this study, that theme is women, their characteristics, and, more particularly, their vices and virtues.

The *Contenance des fames,* the *Bien des fames,* and the *Blasme des fames* may be regarded as light verse, a genre that encompasses a wide variety of poetic forms in which the poet assumes a whimsical or satirical attitude toward the subject. Light-verse subject matter may be sophisticated or trivial; it may be narrow in focus, or, as in the case of these three *dits,* universal. Light verse usually treats its themes in a sportive, conversational, even bantering manner. Less trenchant than the *fabliau,* the *dit* more closely resembles *vers de société,* a kind of light verse that deals with the manners and customs of polite society. As with most light verse, the *dits* in this volume are structured formally, using eight-syllable lines in rhymed couplets; but they do not adhere strictly to this metrical pattern. Frequently they fall into a conversational and singsong cadence. Terse and idiomatic, they are occasionally marred by unimaginative word choice and repetition. At its worst, some of the verse is doggerel; at its best, it is crisp, direct, and personal. Clearly these poems were meant to be spoken. Their rapping rhythms and unaffected phrasing must have made them readily accessible to the average medieval listener; they should be equally accessible to contemporary readers who live in an age dominated by a wide variety of informal and street-bred genres.

To convey the tone of the poems, we have tried to preserve their informal language. Even so, our modern English translations may not always render the original faithfully. In a few cases, it has been impossible to determine the exact meaning of a word or term. Further, our effort to retain the couplet structure (though not the octosyllabic meter) has forced us to take some liberties with word choice. Word patterns such as the serial repetition of phrases, deliberately introduced to serve the poet in oral performance, have been retained. Our overall aim has been to capture the spirit of the poems. Wherever we have deviated from the original, the literal translation appears in the notes following each poem. The asterisks in the English translations refer the reader to the notes following each text.

In the essays that precede these *dits* we have attempted to reanimate the past by setting the poems in their historical and literary contexts. The *dits* present some challenges to linguists, historians, and specialists of French literature. They depart from standard definitions of high art in that they are neither elevated in subject matter nor refined in style. Unlike low art, however, they are neither crude nor lacking in sophistication. They do share with the *fabliaux* a frank and idiomatic tone, a tell-it-like-it-is spontaneity, and a vocabulary that addresses secular concerns and everyday matters. Still, it is difficult to fix the intent of our authors. Did they mean to tell the truth with a laugh (as Horace described satire)? Did they deliberately distort for the sake of humor? Although all literature reshapes reality, satiric literature and parody have a critical intent, and our poets did moralize even as they entertained.

In constructing this book, we have presented one pro-female poem with two anti-female ones in order to mirror the medieval polemic concerning the role of women in society. The greater space given to the anti-female material in our discussions reflects the misogynic tradition that prevailed in medieval times and subtly persists into our own age. Since, according to Webster's dictionary definition, the word *feminist* refers to one who advocates the political, economic, and social equality of the sexes or generally defends the rights and interests of women, we have avoided the words *pro-feminist* and *anti-feminist,* preferring instead *pro-* and *anti-female.*

Translated into modern English, these poems enlarge the fund of medieval documents available to specialists and nonspecialists alike. Their numerous references to medieval customs, manners, and fashions make them particularly valuable to historians and broaden our understanding of medieval attitudes toward women.

Acknowledgments

The production of *Three Medieval Views of Women* has been a cooperative effort. Gloria K. Fiero conceived the idea for the book and explored the historical background of the poems. Wendy

Pfeffer transcribed the *dits* from the original manuscripts, edited and collated them preparatory to translation, and provided the linguistic apparatus. Mathé Allain offered important insights into the history of specific words and terms. All three shared in the English translations and in the preparation of the notes to each poem.

Among the many individuals to whom we owe special thanks are: Constance H. Berman, Allen D. Barry, Gregory Clark, Richard C. Cusimano, James H. Dormon, Pierre Kunstmann, Monique Léonard, JoAnn McNamara, Brian Merrilees, Rupert T. Pickens, Carter Revard, Phyllis B. Roberts, Samuel N. Rosenberg, A. George Rigg, Nathan H. Schwartz, Stephen M. Taylor, and Ralph V. Turner. For their assistance toward completion of this project, we are grateful to the Isaac Walton Killam Foundation, the American Philosophical Society, Lydwine Saulnier-Pernuit of the Musées de Sens, the University of Louisville's Committee on Academic Excellence, Arts and Sciences Research Committee, and Graduate Research Committee, and the staffs of the following libraries: the Institut de Recherche et d'Histoire des Textes (Section romane), Paris; the Bibliothèque nationale, Paris; the bibliothèques municipales in Dijon, Besançon, and Rouen; the British Library, London; the University Library, Cambridge; the Bodleian Library, Oxford; the Muniment Room and Library, Westminster Abbey, London; and the Biblioteca Laurentiana, Florence.

Three
Medieval
Views of
Women

WENDY PFEFFER

The *Dits:* The Genre, the Texts, the Language

The *Dit*

As medieval authors and scribes were less interested in defining genre than are modern scholars, no medieval definition of the *dit* exists. But there are works identified as *dits* in medieval manuscripts, either by title (the *Blasme des fames* is called the "Dit de la condition des femmes"[1] in the Westminster manuscript) or in the work itself. The anonymous author of the *Dit des boulangers,* for example, begins his work:[2]

> J'ai mainte parole espandue
> et mainte maille despendue
> et dedenz taverne et en place
> encor ferai cui qu'il desplace
> quar s'on me chace je fuirai
> et s'on me tue je morrai
> mes ainz voudrai sanz contredire
> des boulengiers un biau dit dire.   [lines 1–8]

(I've spread many words and spent many coins both in taverns and in the [market]place, and I'll do it still whomever it may displease. For if someone chases me, I'll flee; if someone kills me, I'll die. But now I want, without contradiction, to tell a handsome *dit* about the bakers.)

Dits tend to be descriptive rather than narrative. The word *dit* seems to mean "something said," and, indeed, the lines from the *Dit des boulangers* indicate that this author recited his works aloud in taverns and town squares. Many *dits* describe the crafts of the medieval city, such as the *Dit des boulangers* (bakers), the *Dit des bouchers* (butchers), the *Dit des changeors* (moneychangers), the *Dit des tisserands* (weavers). The *Dit des moustiers* lists all the churches of Paris in the year 1323; another lists the equipment needed for a household (*L'Oustillement au vilains*).[3] This characterization applies to *dits* written in the late twelfth and thirteenth centuries, but the genre seems to have changed as time progressed. Fourteenth- and fifteenth-century authors use *dit* to refer to longer works less descriptive and more narrative in nature.

The subject of our poems is women, a topic treated in a number of *dits,* including the *Dit des cornetes,* which criticizes feminine headdress, and the *Pie et la femme,* which compares woman to a magpie. Similar to our two anti-female texts in theme and imagery are the *Epystle des fames* by Jehan Durpain, the *Evangile des femmes,* and the *Blastange des femmes.* In addition to the *Bien des fames,* there are at least two other *dits* which praise women, a *Dit des femmes* and a piece called the *Bounté des femmes.*[4]

All these texts, regardless of their subject matter, are relatively short. The *Blastange des femmes* has 84 lines, our *Bien des fames* has 96, the *Contenance* has 176, and one version of the *Blasme des fames* has 190 (Florence, Biblioteca Laurentiana, Plut. XLII 41). The metrical pattern for *dits* seems not to have been fixed, but the octosyllabic couplet, the meter used in the three poems presented here, seems to have predominated. An octosyllabic couplet is formed by two rhyming lines of eight beats each. Though the two lines are tied to one another by rhyme, the authors of our *dits* did not constrict their thoughts to two-line groupings. The author of the *Contenance des fames,* for example, regularly allows his thoughts to run past the end of one couplet into the next. The author of the *Blasme des fames* is the least conscientious in terms of the octosyllable; versions of his text in both manuscript families (see below) show irregularities in meter—that is, there are verses too long or short by a syllable or two.

Establishing a Text

Establishing the text of a *dit* is a delicate task since, like the *Dit des boulangers*, most were composed for oral recitation. Frequently the words were not written down until well after the piece was composed and performed, and most often not by the author. Rather, a professional scribe would copy the text by hand either from memory or while the author recited it aloud. Once the text was written down, other scribes could copy it. Although certain texts were rarely changed—Latin versions of the Gospels, for example—others were subject to alterations for a host of reasons. For example, a scribe working in England but copying a text composed in Paris would be inclined to change spellings to reflect his own pronunciation (as though an American southerner were to read the word *you* and copy it as *y'all*). The *Blasme des fames* exemplifies this tendency: the *dit* was originally written in a continental French dialect, but we have three versions of the text in Anglo-Norman, the dialect of French spoken in England in the Middle Ages.

Or a scribe may have felt creative and added to the text, drawing his material from another work (as did the scribe who appended lines from the *Blasme des fames* to the *Quatre Souhaits de Saint Martin*) or creating his own verses, a fact that explains differences in length in different versions of the same text (the versions of the *Blasme des fames* vary from 76 to 190 lines). Each of the texts presented here exists in more than one copy, no two of which are identical. Even a short text, with only three medieval copies, such as the *Bien des fames,* shows differences.

Sometimes it is possible to reconstruct scribal behavior, and thereby to determine something of the history of a manuscript. For example, the two Paris manuscripts and the Oxford manuscript of the *Blasme des fames* include the couplet: "plus a en fames males teches / que il n'a en la mer de seches" ("There are more bad qualities in women / than there are cuttlefish in the sea.")[5] But the scribe of the Westminster text did not think his readers would understand what *seches* (cuttlefish) meant and substituted a word he thought they would know, *places:* "que il n'a en la mer de places" (line 126: "than there are plaice in the sea"). We can be fairly sure that the original text used *seches* because three manuscripts have it (opposed to one manuscript with *places*) and because *seches* rhymes with *teches* while *places* does not.

The editor of a medieval text must decide how to present the piece he is working with. An editor can try to determine which manuscript is the oldest and, in theory, the closest to the "original." The oldest copy extant is not necessarily the best version, however. Any number of copies may have been destroyed between the thirteenth century and the present. A more recent copy, for a host of reasons, may better preserve the original author's text. In picking a manuscript for an edition, editors try to build a family tree, called a *stemma,* for the different "witnesses" or versions of a same text. ("Witness" is a better term than "version," because it implies an equality of testimony that "version" does not. Each witness, each medieval copy of a text, allows us a peek at what the author's original might have been. But each witness also has its own history—a scribe who was careless, an owner who erased lines, a vandal who damaged the manuscript by cutting out the illustrations. All these factors enter into an editor's thoughts as he works with the text.) The stemma, if properly constructed, allows an editor to see the relationships among the different witnesses, and he may try to use them to reconstruct the author's original, or something close to it. Alternatively, he may accept the testimony of one witness as it has come down to us today, making as few changes as possible.

A manuscript is usually identified by the city in which it now resides, the library that houses it, the name of the collection to which it belongs, and a classifying number. Once an editor has provided all this information, he may abbreviate, referring to "Paris, Bibliothèque nationale, fonds français 837" as "Paris 837," for example. Within a manuscript, one does not speak of pages with numbers, but rather of folios (abbreviated f.) which have a front (recto, abbreviated r) and a back (verso, abbreviated v): a manuscript with one hundred folios would have two hundred pages.

Our three texts are represented in a total of twelve different manuscripts, now found in places as distant from each other as Florence, Italy, and Cambridge, England. Three manuscripts contain two of our *dits:* the *Blasme* and *Bien* are both found in Paris 837 and Rouen 671, the *Blasme* and *Contenance* in Paris 1593. And it would seem that the *Bien* was once included in this manuscript as well. On f. 168v a new piece is announced, "Ci commence li biens del fames," but no text follows. More than two columns have been erased (room enough for the ninety-odd lines of the *dit*), and f. 169 provides the title of the next piece.

A number of the other manuscripts contain texts similar in their criticism of women to the *Blasme des fames* or the *Contenance,* for the misogynic tradition is far more strongly represented in medieval literature than the pro-female argument. It is, therefore, small surprise that the *dit* praising women is found in relatively few manuscripts — there are only three extant copies of the text.

The *Contenance des Fames*

The Manuscripts of the *Contenance des fames*

Besançon, Bibliothèque municipale 592, f. 17v
Dijon, Bibliothèque municipale 525 (ancien 298[2]), f. 113r
Paris, Bibliothèque nationale, fonds français 1593, f. 107r
Paris, Bibliothèque nationale, fonds français 12483, f. 40v

The *Contenance des fames* exists in four manuscripts. In the Dijon manuscript this *dit* is called "L'epistre des fames"; the Besançon manuscript does not provide a title; the two Paris manuscripts give the title scholars have adopted, "Contenance des femmes."[6] In medieval French *contenance* can mean "conduct" or "bearing," as well as "face," "expression," or "appearance."[7]

The *Contenance* occurs in Paris 1593, a manuscript famous for its collection of *fabliaux* (short comic and frequently ribald tales) and of works by the poet Rutebeuf (fl. 1250–80). It also contains a section of the *Roman de Renart, Fables* of Marie de France, and other *dits,* notably the *Blasme des fames.*

Another manuscript of this text, described in detail by Arthur Långfors, Paris 12483,[8] is known as the "Rosarius" because its anonymous compiler consciously created a "rosary" of pieces in honor of the Virgin Mary. He divided the volume into two sets of fifty chapters, each of which includes a description of an element of natural history, followed by a comparison of this element with the qualities of the Virgin Mary. Then the compiler added one or two pious stories (a saint's life or a miracle of the Virgin); finally comes a song or short work, such as a *dit.*[9] Included in this manuscript are excerpts from the *Testament* of Jean de Meun, and again works by Rutebeuf. We know the anthology was put together after 1328, because one of the pieces included, the *Dit du roi* written by Watriquet de Couvin and dedicated to Philippe de Valois, could not have been written before Philippe's coronation that year.[10] Långfors maintains that the Paris manuscript was copied shortly after this date.[11] If Långfors is correct, the *Contenance*, which is included in this manuscript, must have been composed before 1328/29. An exceptional feature of this collection of texts is that the compiler attempted to identify the authors of the various pieces he included. When the author's name is known, it appears next to the piece; if the compiler himself was the author of several lines of verse, he noted in the margin: 'Ros'; if the author was unknown to the compiler, he marked the piece 'Quid' for *Quidam,* "someone" in Latin. The author of the *Contenance des fames* was unknown to the compiler, who introduced the text with these lines:

> Des mignotises vous dirai
> Et des contenances des dames;
> Combien que soient preudefamez
> Il i a trop de mignotise
> Uns trubers einsi le devise:
> S'uns hons quenoissoit l'avantage . . . [f. 40r –40v]

(I will tell you of the coquetry and the conduct of women; however worthy they may be, there is too much affectation [in them]. A trouvère puts it this way, "If men understood the advantage").[12]

The *Contenance* is also included in a Dijon manuscript, now numbered 525. For this manuscript we know the name of one copyist, Mathias Rivalli, who entered the dates 1355, 1361, and 1362 at the ends of three different pieces. The manuscript contains several works by Jean de Meun, notably the *Roman de la Rose* and his *Testament* and *Codicille,* a French translation of Boethius, and the letters of Abelard and Héloïse in Latin. One is tempted to describe this manuscript as a collection of anti-female pieces, though Boethius's *Consolation of Philosophy* does not fit that description. This manuscript suffered damage sometime before 1802: several folios were torn out of the volume and twenty-six mini-

atures were cut out.[13] One of the latter was on the back of a folio of
the *Contenance;* removal of the miniature resulted in the loss of
eleven lines from our text.

The fourth manuscript is significantly later. Besançon 592 was
copied in the fifteenth century. The first two folios contain poems
on the death of the count of Salisbury, who was killed in 1428,
indicating that the manuscript must have been copied after this
date. This manuscript is written on paper rather than parchment;
the handwriting is not a neat "book hand," but a relatively hard-
to-read cursive script. All the texts of this small book (twenty
folios) are parodic or satiric in nature, whether in French or Latin
—an example included is a parody of the New Testament, the
Evangilium secundum marcam auri et argenti (f. 10v), the "Gospel
according to the mark of gold and silver."

In the nineteenth century, the *Contenance des fames* was printed
by Jubinal, who used a text based on Paris 1593.[14] The text pre-
sented here is that of the Dijon manuscript, except for eleven lines,
where the Dijon text was damaged by excision, supplied from Paris
1593. We have adopted Jubinal's naming of the text (the title
provided by the Paris manuscript), which has been generally ac-
cepted by scholars.

The *Bien des Fames*

The Manuscripts of the *Bien des fames*
London, British Library, Harley 4333, f. 114r
Paris, Bibliothèque nationale, fonds français 837, f. 193r
Rouen, Bibliothèque municipale 671 (ancien A. 454), f. 255v

The *Bien des fames* is so named only by the Paris manuscript.
The Rouen text bears no title; Harley 4333 calls the piece "L'epis-
tre des fames." Since there exists in medieval manuscripts a very

different anti-female *dit* called *L'Epistre des fames*,[15] it is preferable to refer to our pro-female *dit* as the *Bien des fames*, a title which has the additional merit of stating clearly the subject and point of view of the text.

One of the three manuscripts containing the *Bien des fames* is Paris 837, a thirteenth-century manuscript containing many short works in Old French, notably a number of *fabliaux*, but also short stories (*contes*), allegorical narratives such as the *Jugement d'Amours*, plays like the *Miracle de Théophile*, works by the poet Rutebeuf, as well as other *dits*, including the *Blasme des fames*. A facsimile of this manuscript was published by Henri Omont.[16] The text of the *Bien des fames* found in the Paris manuscript appeared in print in 1842.[17]

A second manuscript is in Rouen, (671, formerly A. 454). According to Paul Meyer, this manuscript was written at the end of the thirteenth or beginning of the fourteenth century[18] and before the French Revolution was the property of the Abbey of Saint Ouen in Rouen. The 335 folios contain primarily theological works in Latin by authors such as Bernard of Clairvaux and Saint Anselm. But inserted into this anthology are twelve works in Old French, mostly religious in nature—two sermons and an explanation of why one should fast on Fridays, for example. But Rouen 671 also contains the *Bien des fames* and the *Blasme des fames*, no doubt included to provide additional material for sermons.

The third manuscript containing the *Bien des fames* is Harley 4333, in the British Library, London. Paul Meyer identified it as a manuscript from eastern France and dated the volume to the second half of the thirteenth century.[19] This manuscript contains Old French works of a didactic nature, from the *Fables* of Marie de France to a French *Ave Maria*, as well as the *Bien des fames*, paired with a text critical of women, the *Evangile des femmes*.

The folios of Paris 1593 (see above for description) that once

contained a text entitled the *Bien des fames* have been so com-
pletely erased that none of the text can be read, even under ultra-
violet light. Were it not for the rubric, which was not erased, it
would be impossible to know that this manuscript once contained
the text. Given the length of the erased passages, it is likely that the
text erased from this manuscript was another version of our *dit*.

The three manuscripts (Paris, London, and Rouen) present basi-
cally the same text of the *Bien*. Analysis of the relationships among
the three manuscripts is reflected in the following stemma:

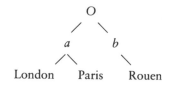

This stemma indicates that the London and Paris texts are close-
ly related, while the Rouen text is more distant. The stemma is
based on several suppositions. At the apex stands the now lost
original (O). It is assumed that two, now lost, copies were made of
this original (identified by lowercase letters); that Paris and London
were copied from the same, now lost, manuscript (*a*) and that
Rouen was copied from the other lost manuscript (*b*).

A careful examination of the three extant versions, line by line,
substantiates this stemma. Here, only "substantial differences"—
that is, differences of vocabulary beyond the substitution of syn-
onyms, a difference in tense or person of verb, or the inversion of
elements in a phrase—have been considered.

On numerous occasions, the London and Paris versions present
the same text where Rouen diverges (for example, at lines 36, 38,

40, 44; see Variants). Twelve lines shared by London and Paris (49, 50, 57–59, 64, 65, 86, 88–90) are entirely missing from the Rouen version (the text of which is only seventy-four lines long and appears to be incomplete). These differences explain the close relationship on the stemma between the Paris and London manuscripts vis-à-vis the Rouen text.

But it is important to note that there are lines shared by Paris and Rouen (14, 32, 85) that are different from the London manuscript (see Variants), and there are lines shared by Rouen and London that are missing from the Paris manuscript (71–72, 75–76, and 87–88 of our text). There are also instances in which each manuscript provides its own text (48; see Variants). These differences are the result of the transmission of the text by the nonextant manuscripts *a* and *b*. Each time the text was copied, lines may have been changed or lost due to scribal error. When lines are missing from one extant manuscript but are found in manuscripts on different branches of the stemma, those lines probably appeared in the original text.

In an effort to establish a text that comes close to the author's original, or the nonextant text at the apex of the stemma, I have used as foundation the Paris version, whose Francien dialect (French of the Paris region) is, I believe, closer to the original text than the Anglo-Norman dialect of the London manuscript. In addition, the Paris scribe seems to have understood his text slightly better than his counterpart for the London manuscript, as there are several lines where the Paris version is clearer in its meaning than the London one. I have added to the Paris text those lines that are found in both the other two versions (71–72, 75–76, and 87–88) but are omitted from the base manuscript (Paris). I think these lines found in the London and Rouen manuscripts probably appeared in the original.

The *Blasme des Fames*

The Manuscripts of the *Blasme des fames*

Family A

Oxford, Bodleian Library, Digby 86, f. 113v
Paris, Bibliothèque nationale, fonds français 1593, f. 153r
Paris, Bibliothèque nationale, fonds français 837, f. 192v
Rouen, Bibliothèque municipale 671 (ancien A. 454), f. 254r
Westminster Abbey, London, 21, f. 35v

Family B

Cambridge, University Library, Gg I.1, f. 627r
Florence, Biblioteca Laurentiana, Plut. XLII 41, f. 83v
London, British Library, Harley 2253, f. 111r

Our third piece is known as the *Blasme des fames,* the title provided in the two Paris manuscripts (Paris 837 and 1593). Other medieval titles for the work include "Les propretés des femmes en romaunz" (Cambridge), "Tractatus de bonitate et malitia mulierum" (Florence), or the "Dit de la condition des femmes" (Westminster).

Of all the *dits* that discuss women, none is present in as many manuscripts as the *Blasme des fames.* The *Blasme* appears in two manuscripts with the *Bien des fames,* Paris 837 and Rouen 671, and shares a manuscript with the *Contenance des fames,* Paris 1593. But five additional manuscripts exist.

The Cambridge manuscript (G.g. I.1) is an enormous volume of 633 folios; originally the tome was even longer. The manuscript was probably compiled in the first half of the fourteenth century, since it includes a reference to the death of Edward I (d. 1307).[20] Though it is difficult to determine the audience for which this manuscript was intended, the original audience must have known

English, as there are several English texts in the volume. The French or Anglo-Norman works of particular interest to an English audience include a history of Britain (*Le Brut*) and a work by Walter of Bibbesworth for English-speakers who wanted to learn French. A Harley manuscript in London, 2253, also contains the *Blasme des fames*. This manuscript is usually described as a "miscellany," for it includes saints' lives, love lyrics, *fabliaux*, a guide to pilgrimages in the Holy Land—prose and verse in French, Latin, and English. It is famous for its English lyrics, known as the "Harley lyrics." The manuscript was published in facsimile by N. R. Ker;[21] our text appeared in print in an edition by Thomas Wright and in a diplomatic edition by Thomas Kennedy.[22] Carter Revard has argued that Harley 2253 is a carefully compiled anthology put together by a scribe knowledgeable in legal and academic matters for a similarly knowledgeable audience.[23] The manuscript was copied by a scribe who worked in and around Ludlow, in southern Shropshire, between 1314 and 1349. Comparisons with date samples of his handwriting suggest that Harley 2253 was copied for the most part during 1340–41, though its last folios are perhaps from 1343–47.[24]

One of the oldest manuscripts in which the *Blasme* appears is Digby 86, currently located in the Bodleian Library in Oxford. This manuscript, which was written after 1272, and possibly before 1283,[25] contains texts in English, Latin, and Anglo-Norman. The contents of this manuscript were published by Stengel in 1871.[26] Tacked on to the *fabliau Les Quatre Souhaits de Saint Martin* are some thirty-six lines from our text, interrupted by twenty-one lines, equally critical of women, in a different meter.[27]

Another manuscript of the *Blasme des fames,* again in London, is Westminster 21. According to Meyer, this manuscript was produced in France toward the middle of the fifteenth century and transported to England shortly afterward.[28] Like Besançon 592, discussed above, the Westminster manuscript is written on paper rather than parchment. Based on its watermarks, I believe it was produced shortly after 1434.[29] It contains seventy-six folios, which include courtly lyrics, courtly riddles (the *Demandes amoureuses*), and two works by Christine de Pizan, an early-fifteenth-century French feminist. The contents of this volume imply a female audience, for whom the *Blasme des fames* would serve as a model to avoid.

The Florence manuscript, Pluteus XLII 41, now in the Biblioteca Laurentiana, once belonged to the Medici family.[30] The scribe, Petrus Berzoli of Gubbio, signed and dated his work on this book: the manuscript was completed on March 5, 1310. This version of the *Blasme* was reprinted by Paul Heyse in 1856. It shows Italian or perhaps Occitan influence,[31] not surprising given the contents of the volume, which includes troubadour poetry, lives of the troubadours, an Occitan grammar, and an Occitan-Italian glossary. It is rather curious that at the end of the volume are two works in French, neither of which agrees in theme with the rest of the collection, the *Moralités des philosophes,* attributed to William of Conches, and the *Blasme des fames.*

These eight manuscripts divide into two broad groups or families. The manuscripts in Oxford, Rouen, Westminster, and both Paris manuscripts form "Family A," and the manuscripts in Cambridge, Florence, and the British Library make up "Family B." Within Family A, the Paris 837 and Rouen manuscripts are so close in many of their lines that they appear to have been copied from the same model. Paris 1593 is related to this model, as is the Westminster manuscript. But both Paris 1593 and the Westminster manuscript lack the list of animal similes found in Paris 837 and the Rouen, London, Florence, and Cambridge manuscripts. The Oxford text, only thirty-six lines long, is incomplete but shares a sufficient number of lines with these manuscripts to belong to the same family. Family A, despite its internal differences, is a relatively coherent family: the variations from manuscript to manuscript are relatively slight.

Family B, the manuscripts in Cambridge, Florence, and London, lack lines found in Family A (twenty-seven lines in all), the description of feminine apparel (11–16 in Rouen/Paris 837), for example. On the other hand, these three manuscripts share a total of twenty lines not found in Family A, notably the battle imagery (51–57 and 81–82 in our text). Within Family B, there are significant differences. The Florence manuscript has sixty-eight lines not found in any other manuscript and shares fifty-five lines with the Cambridge manuscript that do not appear in any other witness. Although these three manuscripts are related, the family is not nearly as uniform as is Family A.

Choosing a text for this edition was difficult. Among the manuscripts of the *Blasme des fames,* two from Family A have been published, Paris 1593[32] and the Oxford fragment.[33] From Family B, the Florence manuscript has appeared in print,[34] while the Harley text has appeared both in facsimile[35] and in a printed edition.[36]

The manuscript chosen for this edition is the Cambridge text, which has never been published. It includes one of the longest versions of the *Blasme,* and, though it omits the lines on wearing apparel (see Appendix), it includes the animal similes found in most other versions. The unpublished Family A manuscripts do not differ significantly enough from the Family A texts already in print to warrant publication, while the Cambridge manuscript presents important variants from the published versions. Furthermore, the Cambridge text was written in Anglo-Norman. Three of the manuscripts of the *Blasme des fames* were composed in this dialect of

Old French (London, Oxford, and Cambridge); a fourth manuscript (Westminster), though not written in Anglo-Norman, arrived in England shortly after being compiled, facts which indicate a large English audience for the *Blasme*. With publication of the Cambridge text, all three Anglo-Norman manuscripts will be in print, allowing a ready comparison of these different versions of the same text.

Dating the Poems

The language of our *dits* and the evidence of the extant manuscripts indicate that the three poems date from the late thirteenth to the early fourteenth century, with none originating later than roughly 1328, the date Långfors gives to the Paris 12483 manuscript of the *Contenance*.[37] Two of the *Bien* manuscripts (London and Paris 837) were produced before 1300.[38] Paris 837 also contains a version of the *Blasme* from Family A, whose other manuscripts are predominantly late-thirteenth-century versions. The only firmly dated manuscript containing a complete version of the *Blasme* is that in Florence (Family B), which is signed and dated 1310, although the manuscript containing a fragment of the *Blasme* (Oxford, Digby 86, of Family A) has been dated to between 1272–83. None of the texts provides internal evidence for more precise dating, and we must be satisfied to place our three *dits* in the last quarter of the thirteenth century and first quarter of the fourteenth.

The Language of Our Texts

The texts of these *dits* are presented here in the dialects of their respective manuscripts, Francien for the *Contenance des fames* and the *Bien des fames,* Anglo-Norman for the *Blasme des fames. Fran-*

cien is the term applied to the dialect of French spoken in the Paris region in the Middle Ages. Although it was not a literary dialect in the twelfth century, when the first works of medieval French literature were written, by the thirteenth century more and more works were being composed or copied in Francien, as Paris grew in importance both as a university city and as the administrative center of what is now France. The growing importance of Paris was such that the city imposed its speech on the rest of France; the language spoken in France today is the descendant of Francien.

Anglo-Norman describes the dialect of French used in England after the Norman Conquest (1066) when French was the official language of England. Anglo-Norman evolved differently from Francien. In the early Middle Ages, Old French divided nouns into two groups (cases), depending on whether the noun functioned in the sentence as a subject or as the object of a verb or preposition. The disintegration of this two-case system of Old French occurred earlier in Anglo-Norman than on the continent.[39] In our text of the *Blasme des fames,* this disintegration shows in the confusion of the nominative and accusative relative pronouns *qui* and *que* (see lines 90, 95).[40] In Anglo-Norman, the verb endings were similar to those used in western dialects of Old French (*-um* for the first person plural, lines 124, 128). In England these forms remained in use, even as the Francien endings (*-oums,* line 126) gained ground.[41]

Anglo-Norman pronunciation also varied from that of France. While it is difficult to determine how words were pronounced when we have only written texts as evidence, still, in words with a nasalized /a/, like the modern French sound in *blanc,* we think Anglo-Norman speakers tended to round this sound to a nasalized open *o* (modern French *bon*). This difference in pronunciation is represented in Anglo-Norman spelling by -aun-,[42] hence *saunz* (line 4 of the *Blasme*) for *sans,* or *savaunt* (line 51) for *savant* (other examples: lines 50, 52, 82, 108, 114, and the title in the Cambridge manuscript). This divergence in spelling has survived in a number of modern English words of French origin, such as the English *gauntlet* for modern French *gantelet,* or *haunch* for French *hanche.*

However, consistency in spelling is not to be expected in medieval French texts, and is even more unexpected in Anglo-Norman ones.[43] Medieval scribes had no dictionaries to turn to, and spelling variants are found in all of the texts presented here. Thus the *Blasme des fames* uses *saunz* in line 4, but *senz* and *sanz* five lines later.

Anglo-Norman texts are also inconsistent in observance of meter, notoriously so,[44] and this version of the *Blasme* is no exception. At lines 11–12, 127–30, and 144, the scribe slips into decasyllabic lines (ten syllables long), and at lines 60–62 he includes lines of only six syllables. Lines are randomly too long or too short by one syllable. No attempt has been made to regularize the meter of this text, nor have I corrected the French even where the scribe confuses the gender of nouns (98, 106).

The texts of the *Contenance des fames* and *Bien des fames* are less interesting dialectally than that of the *Blasme,* for they are written in Francien. These two texts present few, if any, traits from other dialects. The use of *biaus* in the *Bien des fames* (64) is perhaps a trace of a northern dialect,[45] though this spelling could also represent Anglo-Norman pronunciation.[46] By the same token, a spelling such as this would not be foreign to Parisian readers and might even represent Parisian usage.[47] In terms of the morphology of the *Bien des fames,* the text represents normal Francien usage of the thirteenth century, with the possible exception of *la seue honor* (96). This stressed form of the possessive gave way in the course of the thirteenth century to *la sienne,* so that the usage in our text represents a slight archaism.[48]

The text of the *Contenance* provided here, from the mid-fourteenth-century Dijon manuscript, shows some orthographic and linguistic features that mark its language as slightly later than that of the *Bien* or the *Blasme*. The use of the letter *y*, for example, developed in the thirteenth century,[49] at first to distinguish *i* from *m*, *n*, or *u*, letters that were easily confused in thirteenth- and fourteenth-century handwriting (lines 2, 68, 103 of the *Contenance*). At roughly the same time, *y* began to replace *i* when this letter was the prepositional pronoun (modern French *y*, 152) and to replace *i* as the last letter of a word (examples in the *Contenance* occur at lines 17, 83, 96, 100, 173, 174).

For these texts, the spellings of the manuscripts have been maintained. However, where medieval scribes failed to differentiate between *u* and *v* and *i* and *j*, I have used letters consistent with modern French usage. For example, where the scribes wrote the first-person subject pronoun *ie*, I have written *je*. Where the scribe used *y*, that letter has been retained except where it represents *j* (particularly in the case of line 89 in the *Contenance des fames*). Ordinal numbers have been expanded, so that the manuscript's *.i.* becomes *un* or *une* as the case may be (*Contenance*, 27, 28, 111). All punctuation has been added. Accents have been added only where necessary to understand the text.

Aside from some words that have disappeared from modern French (*moult* replaced by *beaucoup*, for example), French of the medieval period is not that difficult. The grammar of these texts is not substantially different from modern French usage. The two-case system of the twelfth-century language has all but disappeared from these mid- to late-thirteenth-century texts. The orthography of these texts may cause the most difficulty for the modern reader, who must remember that medieval scribes had no dictionaries to consult.[50]

The *Dits* as Literature

The three texts of this volume are notable for the use of a variety of rhetorical devices. Their authors probably had received some

formal education—training in Latin grammar, in logic (consider
the argumentation in the *Bien*), and in rhetoric. Several medieval
authors, notably Matthew of Vendôme and Geoffrey of Vinsauf,
wrote textbooks on rhetoric, and our anonymous poets seem to
have followed their recommendations on a number of occasions.

For example, highly recommended in the medieval textbooks is
repetition, used by the author of the *Blasme* to impress his argu-
ment on the listener. In his long list of animal similes (69–88), for
example, he begins each comparison with the same phrase, "Feme
est. . . ." Such repetition at the beginning of successive lines is
known as *anaphora* or *repetitio*.[51] So, too, the author of the
Contenance repeats "Or," in close to sixty lines of verse (3–61).
Even in the *Bien* we find repetition for the sake of argument (at 50–
51). The author of the *Bien* also repeats the word *Fame* at the
beginning of a number of lines to initiate a new thought (49, 52, 54,
63, 69, 71, 77, 80). Though not, strictly speaking, anaphoric, this
repetition is purposeful and is valuable for rhetorical effect. In
some cases, the repetitions may seem less deliberate, even faulty
(for example, *Blasme*, 47–48, 67–68), but this may result from a
scribe's addition rather than from the author's inattention.

As advised in the rhetorical handbooks of the day,[52] the author
of the *Contenance* cites a number of popular proverbs to emphasize
his argument (see Notes). For medieval authors, proverbs served as
stylistic ornaments and as the bearers of a condensed poetic mes-
sage.[53] Proverbs criticizing women were legion, and it is not impos-
sible that the author of the *Contenance* took his inspiration from
proverbs like "Femme se plaint, femme se deult, / Femme est mal-
ade quand elle veult" ("Woman complains, woman suffers, /
Woman is sick when she wishes").[54] One proverb quoted verbatim
by our author, "Qui croit et aimme fole femme / Il gaste avoir et
cors et ame" (175–76), was used frequently by medieval authors.[55]
And though proverbs praising women do exist, the author of the
Bien did not see fit to use them.

Medieval rhetorical handbooks encouraged the use of alliteration, which Matthew of Vendôme calls *paronomasia* or *admonitio*.[56] Alliteration can be found in all three of our *dits,* although least frequently in the *Bien.* Good examples appear in the *Contenance* at lines 28: "Qui ne puet estre en un estage"; 33: "Or est viguereuse, or est vaine"; 46: "Or est marrastre, or est mere"; and 76: "Yra aux vespres et aus veilles." In the *Blasme des fames* an excellent example of alliteration occurs at line 30, "Le foundement de felunie." And the Latin lines that follow the *Blasme* also exploit this figure of speech, notably in lines 146–47: "longum languorem. lacrimas cum lite dolorem. / pondus valde grave. verbosum vas sine clave."

The rhyme patterns of these *dits* are varied and frequently skilled. Instead of having each couplet "end-stopped," that is, expressing a complete thought, the author of the *Contenance* often does not end his sentence with a closed rhyme but continues his thought into the first line of the next couplet (see 23–24, 65–66, 77–78, 91–92, 133–36, 139–42, 151–54, 157–60). While the three poets often use simple rather than complex rhymes, occasionally richer rhymes appear. The *Contenance* in particular has a number of three-syllable, or leonine, rhymes, such as occur at lines 3–4, 29–30, 107–08, 157–58. The author of the *Bien* has a fondness for "equivocal rhymes," where a single word with different meanings rhymes with itself (9–10, 61–62, 89–90). Of the three *dits,* the *Blasme* is the least complex in terms of rhyme: most of its lines end in one-syllable rhymes.

The misogynic tradition was so prevalent that our authors frequently parallel each other's phrasing. In both the *Contenance* and the *Blasme* women are called quarrelsome, the first text saying "Ore veult paiz, or veult meslee" (52) "Or tensera a sa voisine" (70), the second, "Femme fet fere les turneez" (57). These two texts, with similar themes, emphasize the folly of men who seek female company. The author of the *Contenance* writes, "Qui plus

l'esgarde plus est fol!" (79) and his confrere observes in the *Blasme,*
"Femme afole le plus savaunt" (51) and "Atret li home e puis
l'afole" (68). The stock nature of the anti-female argument is seen
even in the *Bien,* "N'en doit nus dire se bien non" (33), which
parallels "Jeo ne ose de eus si bien non dire" of the *Blasme* (144).

The similarities in wording among the *dits* suggest that our
authors were familiar with a well-established and popular literary
tradition. Lines similar to those found in them appear in other
works of the period, such as the pro-female text that immediately
precedes the *Blasme* in the Harley manuscript.[57] Here again we
read the commonplace, "Pur ce ne dient si bien noun" ("Therefore
they say nothing if not good," 56) and discover statements similar
to those in the *Bien des fames,* such as that all men are born of
woman (73–76), and that "De femmes vienent les pruesses"
("From women comes prowess," 91). The author of the *Bien*
repeats a number of commonplaces in his *dit,* for example, "Que
aus fames honor ne porte / La seue honor doit estre morte" (95–
96), lines found in a number of medieval works, notably in Chré-
tien de Troyes's romance of *Perceval* (539–40: "Qui as dames
honor ne porte, / La soe honor doit estre morte").[58]

The statement that women drive men crazy may be considered
proverbial. This theme (discussed above) appears in the romance
Amadas et Ydoine, when the author seeks to contrast his virtuous
heroine, Ydoine, with her female contemporaries.[59] He observes,
"[Feme] afole que le plus sage / et qui a plus soutil corage ("Wom-
an makes crazy him who is the wisest and has the finest heart,"
3579–80), and again: "Fols est qui en nule se fie" ("He is crazy
who puts his faith in one of them," 3606). The author of this
romance, like the author of the *Blasme,* insists on woman's mali-
cious craftiness:

> Ha! feme, com es enginneuse
> Et decevans et artilleuse,

D'engin trouver puissans et sage,
De bastir mal a grant damage!   [lines 7037–40]

(Ha! woman, how crafty you are, and deceitful and experienced, in
finding powerful and clever tricks to prepare bad to great damage!)

But even this author concludes, "Qu'en doie dire se bien non"
(7068: "That one must only say good [of them]").

In Vatican manuscript Regina Latina 165,[60] another anti-
female text, we read that woman "Hardie est cum leon, e faus
serment fere, / Lange had de serpente, poignant e venimouse"
("She is hardy as a lion and makes false statements / She has a
serpent's tongue, sharp and venomous," 4–5), "Fontaine de tuz
maus e de felonnie" ("A fountain of all ills and of evil," 19), "Ke
l'em dit pur veir, si n'est pas fable, / Ke famme set plus ke deable"
("Let people say truly, it is not a fable / That woman knows more
than a devil," 45–46).

Another anti-female text, the *Evangile aux femmes*, draws on
the same commonplaces.[61] This poem is composed of four-line
stanzas, of which the first three lines praise women, while the
fourth contradicts or inverts the statements of the first three. Lines
of praise and of condemnation echo those found in our *dits*. For
example, the author of the *Evangile* writes, "N'est sages ne cortois
qui de fame mesdit, / Car toute loiauté en eles maint et gist" ("He is
neither wise nor courtly who speaks ill of woman / For all loyalty
lies and rests in them," A 19), only to contradict these words with a
final sally at those so naive as to believe such a statement. Other
lines from this text are reminiscent of our *dits,* as in the comparison
between women and animals: "Humble comme coulon, comme
lyon hardie" ("Humble as a dove, hardy as a lion," 19) or the
attack on the warmongering of women: "Feme est uns anemis qui
fait en petit d'eure / dont trestous uns païs, une contree pleure"
("Woman is an enemy who does in a short time / what makes
whole realms and lands to mourn," A 25).

The most famous vernacular author of the thirteenth century, Jean de Meun, broached similar themes in his contribution to the *Roman de la Rose*, written between 1269 and 1278.[62] The tone of this work is, at times, vehemently anti-female. For example, the character "Nature" comments:

> Trop ont fames en leur courages
> et soutilletez et malices.
> Qui ce ne set fos est et nices,   [lines 18102–04]

(Women have in their hearts / too many ruses and too much malice. / He is foolish and naive who does not know this).

Another speaker, "Friend," repeats the words of a jealous husband on the subject of marriage: "Ne sai don vient ceste folie, / fors de rage et de desverie" ("I do not know where this folly comes from / except from madness and from insanity," 8635–36).

A misogynic tradition existed not only in vernacular literature, but in Latin literature as well. In the late thirteenth century, a cleric named Matheolus wrote a long *Complaint*, in which he decried his married state and the woes marriage had brought him.[63] His poem echoes many of the statements found in our French works. And the *Blasme* concludes with a quotation, considered proverbial in medieval Latin literature,[64] that copies the rhyme scheme of Matheolus's Latin text.

While it is difficult to assess authorial skill in works where scribes clearly played a large role (this is especially true of the *Blasme*), some generalizations may be made. Though not superb stylists, these poets were energetic popularizers who, being familiar with the contemporary literature on their chosen theme, were at ease with the rhetorical tricks of their trade and produced poems that still make enjoyable and entertaining reading.

Notes

1. We have consistently used the spelling "fame" in the titles of our three *dits;* within the texts, the manuscript spelling has been retained: either *fame* or *femme.*

2. This text, never printed, is found in Paris manuscript Bibliothèque nationale fonds français 837, f. 175b.

3. See Paris 1971: 266–86; Schalk 1968: 1:249–53; and the *Grundriss der romanischen Literaturen des Mittelalters* 1970: 2:289–91.

4. Meyer 1877: 499–503.

5. Lines 71–72 of Paris, Bibliothèque nationale fonds français 1593; ll. 93–94 of Rouen, Bibliothèque municipale 671 (ancien A.454); Oxford, Digby 86, f. 113 vb, ll. 36–37.

6. See note 1 above.

7. Burgess 1977: 21, 34.

8. See Långfors 1916.

9. Långfors 1916: 15.

10. Långfors 1918: 1.

11. Långfors 1916: 17.

12. Literally: "If a man knew the advantage." I have used the first line of our text here, a slightly looser translation.

13. Omont 1905: 364n.

14. Jubinal, ed., 1842: 2:170–77.

15. "L'Epistre des femmes" was used as the title of a number of *dits;* the *Contenance* is so dubbed in the Dijon manuscript, the *Bien* in Harley 4333. Scholars today reserve the title for a third *dit,* whose first line is "Femes sont de diverse vie" (Långfors 1970: 142).

16. Omont 1932.

17. Jubinal, ed., 1835: 83–86.

18. Meyer 1883: 76.

19. Meyer 1872: 206.

20. Meyer 1886: 283.

21. Ker 1965.

22. Wright and Halliwell, eds., 1841–43: 2:221–23; Kennedy 1973: 103–18.

23. Revard 1982: 139–43.

24. The discovery of holographs by this scribe was reported by Revard 1979: 199–202, and a recent account of them is given in Cox and Revard 1985: 33–46, esp. 45n15. For the date of the manuscript, see also Ker 1965: xxi–xxii and Parkes 1969. Both Ker and Parkes have concurred in the dates suggested by Revard (Revard 1988).

25. See Gosman, ed., 1982: 61; Miller 1963: 29; also Mihm, ed., 1984: 31.

26. Stengel 1871. For her D.Phil (Oxford), Charity Meier-Ewert prepared an edition of many of the French poems in Digby 86, but I have been unable to consult her work. I thank Carter Revard for this reference.

27. The reference to Saint Martin in the *Blasme* text (which appears in four of the manuscript versions of Family A: cf. "por ce vos di par saint Martin" Paris 1593, l. 67) explains the presence of these lines in the *Quatre souhaits de Saint Martin*.

28. Meyer 1875: 25.

29. Compare Briquet 1968: no. 8485 and nos. 13261–63; 13265, 13268.

30. See the description of this manuscript by the Institut de recherche et d'histoire des textes, section romane.

31. Examples include the rhymes *natura : dura* for *nature : dure* at lines 125–26 of the manuscript text or again *sua natura : ella plus iura* for *sa nature : elle plus iure* lines 165–66.

32. Jubinal 1835: 83–86.

33. Stengel 1881: 38–40.

34. Heyse 1856: 63–71.

35. Ker 1965: 111r–v.

36. Wright and Halliwell, eds., 1841–43: 2:221–23; Kennedy 1973: 103–18.

37. Långfors 1916: 17.

38. Meyer 1872: 206; Omont 1905.

39. Pope 1961: §1246.

40. Ibid. §1262.

41. Ibid. §1272.

42. Ibid. §1152.

43. Ibid. §1205.

44. See Legge 1950: 137–41; Vising 1970: 79–83.

45. Pope 1961: N §viii.

46. Ibid. §1165 (2).

47. Ibid. §659.

48. Ibid. §859.

49. Ibid. §734.

50. Ibid. §518–19. For more information on medieval French, see Raynaud de Lage 1981. For more information on editing manuscripts, see Stiennon and Hasenohr 1982 or Foulet and Speer 1979.

51. Matthew of Vendôme 1981: 80 §5 (Faral 1982: 168); Geoffrey of Vinsauf 1967: 56 (Faral 1982: 231, l. 1098).

52. Matthew of Vendôme 1981: 22 (Faral 1982: 113–14 §16–17); Geoffrey of Vinsauf 1967: 56 (Faral 1982: 201, ll. 126–33).

53. Schulze-Busacker 1985: 60. See Maranda 1974 for a discussion of proverbs as a reflection of medieval French life: "Women [in proverbs] are essentially devils who transform life into hell" (109).

54. Morawski 1925: #739.

55. Ibid. #1877; Schulze-Busacker 1985: 282–84; for the complicated history of this proverb, see Singer 1944–47: 1:15–18.

56. Matthew of Vendôme 1981: 81 §9 (Faral 1982: 169 §9).

57. London, British Library, Harley MS 2253, f. 110v., printed in Wright and Halliwell 1841–43: 2:218–21; diplomatic edition in Kennedy 1973: 95–102.

58. Chrétien de Troyes 1959.

59. *Amadas et Ydoine* 1926.

60. Merrilees, ed., 1971: 6–9.

61. Jodogne, ed., 1959: 1:353–75.

62. Guillaume de Lorris and Jean de Meun 1970–73.

63. Matheolus 1892–1905.

64. See Walther 1966: 23903–04.

GLORIA K. FIERO

The *Dits*:
The Historical Context

Literature is one of the liveliest resources available to historians. As historical documents, the three *dits* that constitute the subject of this book tell us much about the time and place in which they were produced. Though the poems may not always faithfully mirror social realities, they do recount elements of material culture and reflect attitudes and opinions shared by the authors and their audiences. Indeed, the poems reveal as much about the prejudices of those who wrote them as they do about the lives of the women they describe.

During the period when these *dits* flourished—roughly 1275 to 1330—the prestige of medieval French monarchy was at its height. Louis IX (1234–70), canonized at the end of the thirteenth century, had enhanced the power and reputation of the crown by providing France with strong and efficient royal government. Increased centralization under Louis's grandson, Philip IV the Fair (1285–1314), threatened feudal interests by challenging the social and political preeminence of the feudal nobility and eventually caused Philip to clash with the papacy, which was exerting equally energetic efforts to centralize the Church. The last major crusade against the Moslems ended in failure in 1270—King Louis died in one of its last campaigns—but the Crusades themselves had stimulated travel and trade. By the end of the thirteenth century, local and long-range commerce vitalized trade routes and urban centers, most notably Paris. Urban growth was enhanced by the efforts of French monarchs to encourage commercial activity. In medieval towns there emerged a class of merchants and craftspeople—the bourgeoisie—whose values and interests were shaped by commercial advantage and material gain. Benefiting from such growing specialization and long-range commerce, guilds—associations of people in like occupations—multiplied in number and size.[1]

New systems of learning, based on the revival of Aristotelian logic, and educational institutions that fostered the disciplines of law, medicine, and theology, stimulated intellectual debate and supported literary productivity. French kings ordered the collection and codification of local legal customs and practices. The years between 1275 and 1330 witnessed a gradual transition from the dominant forms of early medieval social organization, feudal and manorial for the most part, to a more cosmopolitan, more materialistic, and more complex social order—changes best reflected in the two monumental expressions of medieval urban life: the Gothic cathedral and the university.

The three *dits* that are the subject of our study represent a unique kind of historical text. On the one hand, these poems, like charters, bills of sale, wills, and traditional historical documents, provide information about women of a particular time and place; on the other hand, as works of art they derive in large measure from the poets' personal perceptions and opinions. For this reason, it is difficult to distinguish the ascriptive from the descriptive content of the poems. Secular in subject matter and phrased in an informal and conversational tone, they were probably intended as popular entertainment. But since the *Bien* and the *Blasme* appear together in at least one manuscript that includes sermons, the poems also might have provided materials for the recitations of medieval preachers.

The *dits* resist historical analysis because their authors cannot be identified by sex, age, or class. One manuscript of the *Contenance* notes that a trouvère, that is, a poet from northern France, composed the poem, a fact that does not fix its origin but links it to the courtly literary tradition. As recent research on the class origins of medieval poets indicates, troubadours (the southern counterparts of the trouvères) came from a variety of backgrounds ranging from humble to aristocratic, so widespread was vernacular literacy.[2] Nevertheless, it may be argued that these *dits* were written by, for, and about the upper strata of medieval French society, noble and/or bourgeois. The author of the *Contenance* describes the material wealth of the upper-class woman, her fine clothing, her mobility, and her enjoyment of friends and servants. The *Bien* and the *Blasme* make repeated references to entertainments and activities of the feudal nobility, such as jousts and tourneys (*Bien*, 66–70; *Blasme*, 57–58); the allusions to city life in the *Contenance* and the *Blasme* (which we shall examine presently) suggest that the authors were familiar with upper and middle bourgeois society.

Although women did write in a variety of genres throughout the Middle Ages, the voice heard in these poems implies male authorship.[3] The *dits* carry the mock confidential and hortatory tone of one comrade addressing another (note especially lines 175–76 of the *Contenance*, 1–2 of the *Bien*, and 1–4 of the *Blasme*). Two of the poems are misogynic; that is, they betray attitudes deeply critical and mistrustful of women in general. The assumption that it is the author's prerogative to examine and judge womankind—implicit in all three poems—further supports the hypothesis of male authorship.

It is likely that the authors of the *dits* were university trained, or at least familiar with the methods of reasoned argument practiced by schoolmen like Thomas Aquinas (d. 1274). The author of the *Bien* presents his point of view in a typically scholastic and rhetorical way, organizing his propositions in an orderly "First reason, second reason" fashion (16, 18) and completing his argument with an *ergo* conclusion (90). A similar though less rigidly rhetorical structure governs the style of the *Contenance*. Here the poet opens by promising to portray "female manners, female ways" (18), states his hypothesis (that women are mutable, 14, 20), and follows with a lengthy set of illustrations to support his argument. Finally, the author of the *Blasme* presents his litany of female faults by means of an elaborate set of comparisons between women and lower species of life, a device that looks back to late antique moralizing treatises on natural history, such as the *Physiologus,* medieval encyclopedias, and bestiaries (see notes to the *Blasme*). This tradition was fundamental to the medieval perception of the universe as hierarchic, symbolic, and comprehensible primarily through analogy.

In his diatribe against women, the author of the *Blasme* argues from the general to the specific. He begins with woman's cursed lineage in Eve and her essential wickedness; then he graduates to more specific and negative ascriptive qualities, such as enmity (53–60), perfidy (93–94, 109–12), infidelity (103–04, 119–20), and aggressiveness (115–16). Similarly, the author of the *Bien* organizes his praise of women so that the first part of the poem advances the general and spiritual aspects of womankind (her lineage from the Virgin Mary, her role as mother, her gentleness and humility), while the second part of the poem (beginning at line 63) turns attention to more particular and material aspects: her influence on fashion (63–64), her production of wearing apparel (85–86), her association with music and dance (71–76), her contribution to the beautification of the church (88–89), and her role in sponsoring the entertainments of the feudal court (66–70). Whether or not these anonymous authors were university trained, it is possible to reconstruct their milieu in a general manner.

Despite the steady growth of middle-class wealth, in the year 1300 the richest and most comfortable class was still the feudal nobility. Within that class, which constituted less than one-tenth of the total French population, men assumed leadership in political and military matters, offering loyalty and armed service to members of the high nobility from whom they held grants of land (or fiefs). Male members of the ruling class were bound to each other as protectors and defenders of the medieval social order; their upper-class status was inherited through the maternal or paternal (usually the paternal) line. In medieval France, however, despite differences in regional customs, a woman might inherit and rule land, usually in default of male heirs. In matters of inheritance, a noblewoman's position was normally secondary to a man's: younger sons, for instance, usually inherited land before older daughters.[4] Upon marriage, the property a woman brought to her marriage (her dowry) fell under the control of her husband. Although a woman might manage land in her husband's absence, she did not control her dowry or other properties (including her dower—a specified portion of her husband's estate) unless she became a widow. But, in an age when land was the basis of wealth, women often succeeded to a patrimony either by the demise of all male heirs or by becoming widows. Thus, despite the fact that during the thirteenth century the great feudal families increasingly excluded women from inheritance in order to retain control over as much of the patrimony as possible (hence conserving the authority of the male line),[5] women achieved independence and prominence in matters pertaining to property transaction and landholding and, depending on their status and age, often held positions of social and political importance.[6]

Among members of the feudal nobility, marriages were arranged with an eye to the family's advantage; parents often fixed alliances for children who were still in the cradle. If a marriage was not preplanned, and if the feudal overlord relinquished his right to arrange a marriage for his vassal's daughter, the young woman who inherited land might enjoy the courtship of suitors. By the twelfth century, the Church affirmed that no one could interfere with the right of men and women who wished to marry. This position theoretically undermined feudal and patriarchal control over the conjugal choices of men and women. Once married, a woman became the ward of her husband; she could make contracts only with his consent and could offer legal testimony only under special circumstances. Her public and legal rights were limited and she was subject to the will of her husband, who also held the power to punish her physically. Nevertheless, both spouses exercised certain rights over each other's person: neither could join a monastery, take a vow of chastity, or participate in a crusade without the consent of the other.[7]

During the thirteenth and fourteenth centuries, noblewomen usually married quite young. Their average age at marriage was fourteen to sixteen years, while for men it was some ten years older.[8] Despite high female mortality in childbearing and male mortality in combat, the average life expectancy in the thirteenth century was thirty to forty years, with wives usually surviving their husbands.[9]

In an age of high infant mortality—which nevertheless demanded the production of male heirs—pregnancy and childbirth were both frequent and hazardous. Noblewomen did not usually suckle their offspring but employed the services of wet nurses. The female domain was the house and home, a landed estate, castle, or urban palace, usually shared by the extended family and servants. By the year 1300, women enjoyed greater opportunities for travel than they had previously, and pilgrimages to holy shrines offered popular attractions. Upon the death of her husband, the noblewoman usually acted as guardian of her minor children's inheri-

tance. Widows, often wealthy heiresses in the prime of life, might
have to assume extensive responsibilities in managing feudal lands
and supervising laborers and servants.[10]

Until the thirteenth century there was no great difference be-
tween the kinds of academic education afforded men and women
of the feudal nobility. Such formal training as existed was limited to
elementary reading and writing. But this situation changed as the
newly founded universities, to which women were denied entrance,
provided increasingly sophisticated educational opportunities for
men. The exclusion of women from medieval institutions of higher
learning widened the distance between male and female spheres of
intellectual and professional activity.[11]

The education of the young noblewoman was predominantly
social, but usually included reading in the vernacular. Like men,
women of the nobility learned to hunt early in their lives and
cultivated a variety of equestrian skills. They bred falcons, played
chess and backgammon. At the social gatherings that constituted
the central occasions of court life, they might sing, play musical
instruments, dance, and recite. Medieval guides to deportment and
etiquette (known as courtesy books) dictated that aristocratic
women be gay, playful, and courteous, and that they excel in the art
of entertaining.[12] Young women were usually taught to sew and
embroider, activities considered appropriate for women. A thir-
teenth-century treatise on conduct written by Philippe de Navarre
warns that women should not learn to read or write unless they
intend to be nuns. He argues that love-letters might contain inde-
cent expressions that women and men would never dare to ex-
change by word of mouth. In the *Handbook of Good Customs,* the
early fourteenth-century moralist Paolo da Certaldo advised that
women should make bread, clean capons, cook, launder, spin,
weave, embroider, and make clothes; but he considered learning to

read unsuitable for them unless they were destined for the convent.[13]

Convents offered an alternative lifestyle to upper-class women, providing them with opportunities for education and personal expression that might be denied to women in a noble household. Convent life gave medieval women freedom from male authority (save that of their confessors and priests). Because the nunnery siphoned off daughters of upper-class families unable or unwilling to provide dowries for all of their offspring, it often received women with no special zeal for the religious life. Nevertheless, the convent did offer noblewomen membership in stable and regulated communities in which they might learn to read and write, as well as to copy and illustrate manuscripts, spin, weave, and embroider. By 1300 the number of convents associated with various church-approved religious orders had multiplied, and at the same time women earned greater visibility as mystics, teachers, and saints.[14] The nun's cloistered life constituted a model of chastity, humility, and obedience that was exalted in the literature of the Middle Ages, especially in the sermons and the manuals of instruction for women. The model of the cloistered woman contrasted sharply with the image of the feudal lady presented in the secular literature of the period.

During the twelfth century, a new wave of secular literature patronized by and flattering to women emerged among members of the nobility. Reflecting the romantic aspirations of the leisure class to whom it was addressed, and influenced by a heightened attention to the role of the Virgin as spiritual intercessor and devotional object, courtly literature featured tales of romance and adventure in which a *chevalier*, a knight, performed heroic deeds in order to win the attention and ultimately the affection of a lady, often one already married. The doctrine of *amour courtois*, as codified by the twelfth-century churchman Andreas Capellanus, prescribed specific rules of behavior, a code that dictated the manners and methods of wooing and winning a lady, and it maintained the idea that love in and of itself was ennobling. Andreas writes, for instance, "Love causes a rough and uncouth man to be distinguished for his handsomeness; it can endow a man even of the humblest birth with nobility of character."[15] Such notions are clearly reflected in the *Bien*, which praises the positive effects of a woman's love: "Bien sai que por l'amor des dames / Devienent li vilain cortois; / Nus hom s'il lor disoit anois / Ne puet mie bien cortois estre" ("And the love of a fine lady / Makes the commoner a lord; / For no vilifying bawd / Can become a gentleman," 40–44). Moreover, the transforming power of the lady's love, "makes the coward brave / And ignites the slumbering knave" (55–56). Historically, noblewomen attended the mock battles performed by medieval knights (fig. 1) and bestowed *chapelets d'honneur,* crowns of valour, upon the winning combatants (compare the *Bien,* 73–74). While the *Bien* praises women for prompting "great acts of prowess" (61–62) and for inspiring the contests (jousts and tourneys) that filled the leisure hours of the nobility and provided entertainment for both sexes (66–70), the *Blasme* sees only the negative side. The *Blasme*'s author views "les turneez" (tourneys) as the consequence of woman's penchant for instigating conflict and combat (57–58).

In the *Bien,* the author attributes a civilizing influence to the feudal lady. She protects the rules of *courtoisie* (38–39), the upperclass etiquette associated with good breeding and refined manners. She is the inspiration for songs and dances (71–72), one of which, the *carole,* was a popular ring-style dance usually accompanied by singing (fig. 2). She cultivates the peaceful, bucolic enterprises of wreath-plaiting, feasting, and partying (73–79). Her gentleness subdues wild and mean personalities (49–50); she sweetens the sensibilities of bad-tempered men and cultivates the fine Aristo-

Fig. 1. Men and Women Watching a Joust; Victors Kneel before Women. Detail of ivory tabernacle, Ravenna, 13th century. Ravenna, Museo Nazionale.

telian virtues of moderation and common sense (52–53). If this was the opinion of the author of the *Bien,* it was one shared by women: an anonymous female poet of the late eleventh century advised men to be "duly refined with manners of distinction. / For him who has acquired a name for courtesy like our own, / our maidenly company desires the grace of joy."[16] Medieval women founded monasteries, hospitals, and schools, acted as patrons of the arts, and often set the tone for literature and manners within French society.[17]

In late thirteenth-century French town life, women assumed active roles. Though they held no political positions, they did par-

Fig. 2. Round Dance (*carole*). Ambrogio Lorenzetti. Detail of *The Effect of Good Government*, 1335–40. Fresco, Siena, Palazzo Pubblico.

ticipate in the urban economy that had been vitalized by commercial and banking activities. Townswomen occupied various social levels, their status largely determined by the position of their husbands. The upper-class townswoman shared with her feudal sister many social and legal prerogatives, including inheritance of a portion of her husband's estate. Among artisans, where lineage was not crucial, patterns of inheritance varied, with wives often becoming the principal heirs to their husbands' businesses.

Just as urban life enhanced the position of the lower classes, so it offered women new opportunities in profit-oriented enterprises. Over 150 trade and craft guilds flourished in late thirteenth-century Paris, and in those occupations involving food and clothing, women were especially visible. Guilds devoted to the spinning of silk, the making of elegant head-coverings embroidered with gold and silver thread (known as *chapeaux d'orfroi*) and the embellishing of purses (known as *aumônières sarrazinoises*, see fig. 3) were composed exclusively of women. In guilds dealing with the production and sale of textiles, women were in the majority; they dominated textile-related jobs involving the washing, dyeing, spinning, and weaving of wool and flax (fig. 4) and participated in most aspects of cotton, silk, and lace production. Women were members of guilds that controlled glass cutting, bead making, goldsmithing, manuscript production, and embroidery. Female membership is recorded in eighty-six of the hundred occupations listed by Etienne Boileau in his *Livre des métiers* (c. 1260).[18] Women made ribbons, scarves, wigs, pins, scissors, knives, swords, shoes, and hats. In some of these trades they were trained by their fathers or husbands and simply took over the family business when these male kinfolk died. Nor was it unusual for women to be active in more than one trade. However, no women belonged to the guilds of the great retail merchants, and even the guilds that women dominated were usually supervised by men. Certain occupations, such as carpet-making and the measuring of weights, were male preserves. Nevertheless, women functioned as usurers in medieval Toulouse and were well represented among the coiners at the Paris Monnaie.[19] Some guilds refused membership to women, alleging that they were not sufficiently skilled, while others accepted them only after the demise of their husbands. As guild members, women were subject to the same regulations as men, though on the grounds of modesty city regulations usually prohibited their training male apprentices

Fig. 3. *Aumônière,* silk and gold thread embroidered on linen. French, ca. 1340. Hamburg, Museum für Kunst und Gewerbe.

in their homes. In the early fourteenth century, women's wages were uniformly lower than men's in all professions, with women earning statistically a maximum of 68 percent of men's wages in like occupations.[20]

While feudal society provided little place for the unmarried

Fig. 4. Women Spinning and Carding Wool. *Luttrell Psalter*, English, ca. 1340. London, British Library, Add. Ms. 42130, f. 193.

woman other than in the convent, the town afforded a variety of opportunities for the *femme sole,* the single woman or widow. She might support herself by crafts such as spinning (our English word *spinster* derives from this occupation) or brewing (though women appear to have played a more active role in this industry in England than in France).[21] A woman—single or married—might manage a shop or tavern or assume the responsibilities of a barber, baker, seamstress, money changer, washerwoman, maidservant, wet nurse, bathhouse attendant, or entertainer. A woman's occupation often affected her family responsibilities and legal status. Artisan women, for instance, usually nursed their own babies unless employment made it impossible. A married businesswoman had advantage over a *femme sole* in being able to share responsibilities for debt with her husband.

Urban regulations closely controlled the activities of female prostitutes, who constituted a legally recognized socioeconomic class. Officially sanctioned brothels existed in France from the twelfth century on, and city ordinances confined prostitutes to specific locations and streets. They were not allowed to inherit property and were required to answer to frequent charges of theft, violence, and sorcery.[22]

Women acted as midwives, apothecaries, and surgeons, but they could not practice as licensed physicians because of their lack of university training. Nevertheless, the Paris census of 1292 records the names of eight women physicians (*miresses*). Popular views regarding modesty encouraged ailing women to seek treatment from other women, and in matters of childbirth women almost exclusively took charge; but litigation against successful women doctors who treated both sexes suggests that the medieval medical profession was jealously guarded by its male practitioners.[23]

Women gained greater visibility as laborers during the period under consideration. A comparison of the tax rolls of the late thirteenth and early fourteenth centuries indicates that the number of women in the guilds increased substantially. For instance, whereas the 1292 roll cites eight *fillaresses de soie,* that of 1300 includes thirty-six.[24] Late-thirteenth-century urban women's increasing freedom is reflected in the fact that they were allowed to attend the public bathhouses—there were twenty-six in Paris alone—which earlier had been restricted to males. Bathhouses, however, were notorious sites for illicit assignation and prostitution. The evils of the urban milieu inflamed the moral wrath of medieval preachers, who denounced drunken women, whores, and females whose excessive luxury of dress violated sumptuary laws and religious codes of modesty and decorum.

Women appear in the legal registers of the town courts as defendants against charges of brawling, cheating, beating their servants, robbing tavern customers, as well as for incidents of a more serious nature: adultery, theft, murder, arson, and heresy. Abortion and infanticide were almost exclusively female crimes. The crimes for which medieval women were most frequently convicted, however, were burglary, larceny, and receiving stolen goods.[25] For serious crimes such as murder, women were usually burned at the stake, while male murderers were hanged.[26] In matters of adultery, a double standard also prevailed: had the daughters of the late-fourteenth-century Poitou knight Geoffrey de la Tour Landry committed adultery, they would have been punished by law; yet in the manual he penned for their instruction, their father advised tolerance for and patience with a husband's infidelities.[27] The double standard extended even beyond death: medieval penitentials allowed a bereaved husband to remarry within one month; but a widow was expected to mourn for a full year before she might take another spouse.[28]

The urban environment provided women with more competitive and richly textured lives. Although townswomen played no part in running municipal government, they enjoyed mobility and visibility, taking part in a wider range of religious and cultural events than were available to women of the rural nobility. A courtesy book written by Francesco Barberino between 1307 and 1315 describes the noblewoman as carefully guarded at home, while the middle-class young lady appears frequently on the public streets.[29] The greater variety of opportunities for women in French medieval towns threatened townsmen, who had previously controlled the major positions of economic power. Outbursts of anti-female hostility, such as those that appear in the *fabliaux* and other secular genres, including our *dits,* may be viewed as reactions to women's greater prominence in urban life. Struggles over gender relations were a visible dimension of urban conflicts among mercantile and trade folk—a group less socially homogeneous than the feudal aristocracy, and hence more sensitive to matters of social rank and status.[30]

Of particular concern to the author of the *Contenance* is the secular and materialistic nature of womankind. Twice the author refers to the lady's fondness for jewelry. Like Midas counting his gold, she amuses herself by taking inventory of her possessions: "Ses jouyaux prent, si le[s] remire— /Or les desploie, or les atire." (She takes her jewels out for display— / Spreads them out, hides them away," 103–04). She fears that she will be outdone by her neighbor's jewels (67–68), and that her neighbor might dress better than she (140–41). The *Contenance* here recalls the misogynic sentiments of the twelfth-century scholar John of Salisbury: "Married women make many demands; costly garments, gold and gems, allowance, much furniture. . . . Then night after night a never ending plaint: 'So-and-so is better dressed than I am when she goes out. . . .' "31

The author of the *Blasme* singles out for criticism the greed of women who make beggars of the rich (52). That women are motivated by the desire for material gain is conveyed by lines such as "Femme lui fet mult bele chere / E puis lui fet la luse derere" ("She gives him her good-time routine / Then turns around and shaves him clean," 109–10) and "Femme li tout s'il ad rien" ("She'll strip him right down to his skin" (111), which ascribe predatory characteristics to members of the female sex. Lines 105 to 108 accuse women of ensnaring others for personal profit. Women's dogged perseverance and tenacity, noted in line 92 ("Tut tens bate e tut tens dure"), is closely followed by a reference to women tavern-keepers who cheat their customers (93–94). Women are accused of faithlessness ("Femme ne set estre fel," 97) and of giving bad advice ("Femme doune mauveise consel," 98); but perhaps the most pointed characterization of the materialistic and rapacious female is found in these lines: "E nul ne se puet de lui esgarder / Quaunt ele li vout enginner; / Femme, si ele veut mester, / Nul ne se pot de ceo retrere" ("A man cannot withstand her guile / Once she has picked him for her wile / Her will to power will prevail, / She vanquishes most any male," 113–16). The author of the *Blasme* perceives woman as cunning and formidable, a dangerous adversary. His reproaches may derive from the more broadly ascriptive misogynic topos that warned that "all women are spotted with the vice of a grasping and avaricious disposition, and they are always alert to the search for money or profit;[32] but one cannot help suspecting that he had in mind a particularly aggressive category of urban female.

The liberating effects of the commercial revival and the wealth still enjoyed by members of the feudal nobility were immediately visible in the sartorial domain. In the late thirteenth century, when private wealth was on the rise, men and women of the feudal and urban upper classes sported increasingly luxurious apparel. Flagrant ostentation in dress and overconsumption of wearing apparel were commonplace among the wealthy. The growing preoccupation with outward appearance is reflected in courtesy books like the *Clef d'amours*, which offers numerous details on how to enhance and cultivate attractiveness and even recommends particular styles of dress.[33] The *Contenance* inverts the ideals and values projected in the courtesy literature in that it satirizes the female obsession with physical appearance. The woman described in the *Contenance* thinks only of her public image. She fusses with her hair and head-covering (115–21, 139). She displays herself on the streets: "Or se va monstrier par la rue" (82). She stands in her doorway in order to show off her fashionable clothes (127–28).

This fashion-consciousness of the *Contenance*'s woman has some basis in historical fact. Fashions of the thirteenth century betrayed a new emphasis on travel and mobility. Garments such as the cloak or mantle that were designed for outdoor wear were produced in great numbers.[34] Furthermore, a rapid succession of styles and novel accessories suggest frequent contact among the different parts of Europe. Medieval towns were common locations for the reception and exchange of unusual items of apparel that appeared along with more standard trade goods. Sumptuary laws often included specific proscriptions against fashions from other regions, reflecting a conservative resistance to foreign influences.[35] The purpose of sumptuary laws was twofold: to inhibit material greed and display (in the name of morality) and to maintain class distinctions by regulating the outward signs of class differences. Naturally, the lawmakers failed to accomplish either goal.

The basic garment for females around the year 1300 was the *cotte:* an ankle-length tunic, often laced at the side, with a close-fitting bodice and long, tight sleeves. The *cotte* might be embroidered at the neck and wrists, or trimmed with fur or jewels. Over the *cotte,* a *surcot* was worn; the latter, a long, sleeveless garment with deep-cut armholes, was usually gathered at the waist and might have a variety of lengths or shapes (figs. 5, 6). Before 1240 the *surcot* was usually shorter than the *cotte,* but after the middle of the century, *cotte* and *surcot* were worn at the same length, and greater variations in the style of the *surcot* appeared. The long, full skirt of the garment inevitably had to be lifted to facilitate walking (as well as to display the color and design of the undergarment), and the manner in which the upper tunic was lifted (fig. 7) became an index to the elegance of the lady who wore it.[36] As the author of the *Contenance* remarks in lines 131–33, in lifting the *surcot* the lady deliberately revealed her *cotte* or *pelice,* a fur-trimmed or lined version of the *cotte.* Over the *cotte* and *surcot* a woman might wear a mantle or cloak of heavy fabric, cut wide in a half circle (see figs. 5, 8). The mantle was often secured at the neck by an elaborately ornamented clasp (fig. 8). Like the *surcot,* the mantle might be used as a means of alternately hiding and displaying one's layers of undergarments, as the author of the *Contenance* notes (129).

Fig. 5. The Elect.
Detail of the Last
Judgment. Bourges
Cathedral, ca. 1300.

Fig. 6. Two Couples. *Le Roman d'Alexandre,* Flemish, ca. 1340. Oxford, Bodleian Library, Ms. Bodley 264, f. 138.

Public display of one's apparel was censured repeatedly in sumptuary laws of the thirteenth and fourteenth centuries. In 1298 the city of Narbonne legislated against the warm-weather style of deeply cut armholes in the *surcot* that revealed embroidered parts of the *cotte*.[37] Between 1274 and 1291 the city government of Montauban issued laws forbidding the wearing of certain furs, silk garments, and purple-colored fabrics. Royal ordinances of 1294 forbade members of the middle class, male and female, to wear ermine, precious jewels, and gold or silver crowns, and limited the number of robes that members of the upper and middle class might buy annually. Royal ordinances also attempted to regulate the amount of money various ranks of nobility spent for their garments.[38] The practice of trimming or lining one or more parts of one's costume with silk or fur (fig. 9) became a major issue in European fashion. Regulations issued by many European municipal governments ordered both men and women to wear their outer

Fig. 7. Young Lady Shopping for Belts and Purses. *Manesse Codex*, ca. 1315–30. Heidelberg, Universitätsbibliothek, Ms. Pal. germ. 848, f. 64.

Fig. 8. Yolande de Soissons before an Image of the Virgin and Child. Psalter, French, late 13th century. New York, Pierpont Morgan Library, Ms. 729, f. 232v.

Fig. 9. Woman with a Little Girl. Psalter, English, 13th century. Venice, Biblioteca Marciana, Ms. 2397, f. 13.

garments closed in order to eliminate the deliberate display of fur linings, and certain furs, such as ermine, sable, martin, and miniver, were reserved for royal use. The width of fur borders on garments was restricted, and the prescribed measure was published for use by tailors, who were fined if they violated the law. The Chevalier de la Tour Landry warned that women who owned many fur-lined gowns would be damned for eternity, for the cost of a single gown of this type might clothe forty poor people in wintertime.[39]

A favorite item of display in the female wardrobe was the belt (figs. 5, 7, 9), which was often embroidered with silk thread or encrusted with jewels. From the belt might hang a richly ornamented purse for carrying alms (the *aumônière sarrazinoise,* figs. 3, 7). Revealing one's belt (referred to in line 130 of the *Contenance*) was a common way of proclaiming one's wealth. If the woman herself had ornamented her belt, it advertised her creative talents as well. Women's clothing became more daring around the year 1300. The preference for lower-cut necklines is confirmed in the *Contenance* (80) by the author's complaint that women bare their bosoms and necks for public display.

Early-fourteenth-century extravagance in fashions also included the introduction of multiple colors (*mi-parti*) in a single costume (fig. 2); the purchase of more expensive fabrics, such as brocaded silk and velvet; a taste for greater quantities of fabric for individual garments; and a proliferation in the number of pieces included in a single male or female "outfit." Surely in such fashion-conscious times it was inevitable that the lady, in the words of the *Contenance,* "se tendroit fole et nice / S'el n'est appareillee a droit" ("would never live it down / To be dressed improperly," 134–35). What might be read as mean-spirited ascription may well have been accurate description. For, in fact, the French chronicler Gilles le Muisit recorded (as proof of the growing decadence of early-fourteenth-century fashions) the decided increase in the number of garments in the wardrobes of wealthy men and women.[40] Preaching in thirteenth-century Paris, Gilles d'Orleans vituperated that even the Virgin Mary, a woman of royal blood, would never have considered wearing silk belts and jewelry of the kind fashionable among wealthy women of his parish.[41]

By far the most visible and hence most important part of the medieval female (and male) wardrobe was headgear. Unmarried women usually wore their hair long and unbound, often garlanded with headbands, crowns or wreaths. These might be made of silk, painted paper, flowers, or metal, including gold and silver (fig. 2). The crown (*couronne, chapel, chapellot* referred to in the *Contenance*, 119, 139) and the headband (or *frontel,* 118) were often richly embroidered with jewels. Fixed to this headgear might be a veil, hairnet, ribbons, scarf, or kerchief that would cover or bind the hair (figs. 5, 8, 9). A thirteenth-century inventory from Artois indicates that the best jewels were worn on the crown that embellished a woman's head, and sumptuary laws forbidding the wearing of pearl fillets and crowns made of gold and silver suggest that there was widespread disapproval of such extravagant display.[42]

Other types of headdress covered parts of the face as well as the hair.[43] The wimple (*guimple,* 139), considered a decorous type of headgear, was worn mainly by married women, widows, and nuns. It included a veil that covered part of the head and hung down to the shoulders or was wound around the neck and chin, offsetting the face dramatically (fig. 10). It might cover the woman's face from the brow to the eyes and from the lips to the chin. Women arranged their wimples variously: they might attach them to braided parts of their hair or arrange them to show curls at the ears. Plaits of hair above the ears on either side of the head (fig. 11) gave the headdress a padded or horned look (see *Contenance,* 81, 124 and figs 8, 9). "Horned" headdresses, their protrusions compared

Fig. 10. Woman in a Wimple Gazing in a Mirror. Psalter, Flemish, ca. 1320. Oxford, Bodleian Library, Ms. Douce 6, f. 97.

Fig. 11. Woman at Her Toilet. *Luttrell Psalter,* English, ca. 1340. London, British Library, Add. Ms. 42130, f. 63.

to Satan's horns, became favorite objects of reproach in late medieval poetry and prose.[44] Over the centuries, critics also castigated the female preoccupation with covering and uncovering the face and brow, and with wrapping and unwrapping the head, a reproof echoed in the *Contenance* (120–21; 154–57). In the early third century, Tertullian, a Latin church father, had already asked of women: "What profit . . . do you derive for your salvation from all the labor spent in arranging your hair? Why can you not leave your hair alone, instead of one time tying it up, at another letting it hang loose . . . ?"[45]

The development of more elaborate headgear drew more attention to the appearance of the face. The author of the *Contenance* criticizes women's preoccupation with face-painting (112–13), but he makes no mention of the increasingly popular practice of plucking the eyebrows and temples to emphasize skin tone and bone structure and to produce a fashionably wide forehead. Nor does he refer to the common customs of dyeing the hair and whitening the face with wheaten flour. In the *Contenance,* objection to female face-painting is quite mildly stated, as more a matter of amusement than censure. In fact, the descriptive tone of the *Contenance* suggests the voice of a husband or lover rather than that of a prelate or preacher. By comparison, medieval preachers called cosmetics "the devil's soap," echoing Tertullian's biting castigation that "those women sin against God who annoint their faces with creams, stain their cheeks with rouge, or lengthen their eyebrows with antimony."[46]

Prior to 1300, men's and women's garments were similar, but the fourteenth century witnessed the differentiation of the wearing apparel of the two sexes,[47] with women and men actively competing in matters of sartorial display. Considering that the history of medieval costume indicates that men were as preoccupied with physical adornment as were women, it is difficult to justify the censorious stance the *Contenance* assumes toward female fashion. The historical evidence—sumptuary ordinances and visual resources of the thirteenth and fourteenth centuries—suggests that fashion-consciousness and increased extravagance of dress were on the rise among members of both sexes.

A close reading of the *Contenance* clarifies the context in which the female preoccupation with outward appearance is addressed. It is not vanity itself that the *Contenance* attacks, but vanity as an expression of female mutability and instability. Indeed, in the *Contenance*, fashion-consciousness illustrates the larger theme of female inconstancy. The diatribe launched by the author may be summed up in his general assertion that the moods (and hence the tastes) of women change as often as one blinks one's eyes (110). The captious tone of the *Contenance* springs from the author's image of woman as volatile, erratic, and forever oscillating between dangerous extremes of behavior: "Or est sauvage, or est privee" ("Now she's wild, now she's demure," 51), "Or ne dit mot, et ore parle" ("Now says nothing, now chatters on," 53), and so on. Even as a mother, she is inconstant: "Or est douce, or est amere; / Or est marrastre, or est mere." ("Now she's gentle, now she's tart; / Cruel stepmother, mother sweet of heart," 45–46).

The fickle-female stereotype belonged to a well-established misogynic tradition; in the twelfth century, Andreas Capellanus had spoken at length on the subject: "No woman can make you such a firm promise that she will not change her mind about the matter in a few minutes. No woman is ever of the same mind for an hour at a time. . . ."[48] Almost identical language appears in the *Contenance*: "Feme a un cuer par heritage / Qui ne puet estre en un estage" ("A woman's heart is just not able / To chart a course that's firm and stable," 27–28).

The author of the *Contenance* does not openly censure the mutability of womankind. His description of female restlessness is a tongue-in-cheek reproach mingled with distinct delight in the ornamental aspect of women. His is the tone of the chastising parent who, in describing his child's naughtiness, represses a note of pride. After all, if the upper-class woman in the *Contenance* is vain and spoiled, does not responsibility fall on the men in her life—father, husband, lover—who provide her with the means to indulge her fancies? On the other hand, the *Contenance* clearly condemns various types of immature behavior: frivolousness (14, 153–55, 163), quarrelsomeness (70), and spitefulness (71–72). The author also reproves women for a number of faults—jealousy (66–68, 140–41), pride (129–30), and selfishness (14–16)—traditionally ascribed to women in misogynic literature. These negative forms of ascription derive from the hypothesis (stated in the opening lines of the poem) that men are superior to women. It is to the historical background for this assertion that we now turn our attention.

————∞————

The biological view of women that prevailed well into the modern era was fixed by Aristotle in the fourth century B.C. According to him, the physical universe was composed of form and matter; with reference to procreation, women constituted matter, chaotic and formless, while men provided the life-giving principle of form. As matter deprived of form, the female was an imperfect and incomplete version of the male, related to the opposite sex as mere receiver and inferior instrument.[49] This theory supported the assertions of Greek physicians, including Hippocrates, that the male seed was stronger than the female seed, and that the female was weak and cold by nature. By the end of the third century A.D., the Roman physician Galen asserted that man was biologically the most perfect of animals, even as he was more perfect than woman. This view was still being taught one thousand years later, when medieval university professors lectured students on the biological inferiority of women and warned of the physical dangers presented by them as sexual partners. The popular medical treatise *De secretis mulierum* elaborated on the concept that women were harmful by their very biological nature.[50] And in the second half of the thirteenth century, the great theologian Thomas Aquinas maintained that "a woman is defective and misbegotten, for the active force in the male seed tends to the production of a perfect likeness in the masculine sex; while the production of woman comes from a defect in the active force or from some material indisposition, or even from some external influence, such as that of a south wind, which is moist, as the Philosopher [Aristotle] observes."[51]

The view of females as defective males provided a first principle in the medieval justification for the submission of woman to man, and hence determined the hierarchy of male over female in all aspects of medieval life. The inferiority that men ascribed to women not only deprived the latter of masculine privileges and pre-rogatives, but also operated in more subtle ways to debase their status. For instance, the belief that the father contributed more to conception than the mother justified male authority over offspring. In short, assertions of women's natural inferiority perpetuated the condescending and paternalistic stance found in the *Contenance* and in most misogynic literature.

The opening lines of the *Contenance* state the general assumption that nature gave men the intellectual advantage over women, a condition supporting the author's notion that women are frivolous and weak-minded (1–14), and justifying his diatribe on female mutability (27–28). The author of the *Blasme* attacks women for their childishness (26) and their incapacity to behave rationally (28). The litany of comparisons between women and animals, one of the most entertaining parts of the *Blasme*, accuses womankind of manifesting the worst habits and attributes of the lower forms of life. Woman, as the result of her biological inferiority, is the discordant and rancorous constituent in an otherwise harmonious natural order. She is, in the words of the *Blasme*, "Maudehé ait sa demaine nature," ("accursed by her very nature," 46).

Even the *Bien*, which sings the praises of women, implicitly assumes male superiority. The author urges his comrades *not* to slander or malign women. At the very outset of the poem, as well as at its close, he insists that respectable men incur dishonor by engaging in criticism and abuse of women: "Mes qui los ne pris veut avoir / N'en mesdira por nul avoir" ("Men who seek both honor and praise / Wouldn't slander women's ways," 9–10); and again, "Que aus fames honor ne porte / La seue honor doit estre morte" ("Who leaves their honor unsung, unsaid, / His own honor must be dead," 95–96). In these statements, honor redounds not to women, but to the men who praise them.

The view of womankind advanced by the medieval Church was based in part on the biological argument for women's inferiority. More crucial to the Church's position regarding women, however, was its interpretation of the female role in God's divine plan. In the story of the creation and fall of humankind, recorded in the first book of the Old Testament, that plan was clearly manifest. Genesis reports that God made Adam from the clay of the earth and shaped him in God's own image, whereas Eve was made from Adam's rib. Theologians from Augustine to Aquinas (and well thereafter) believed that the secondary and derivative aspects of female generation proved her inferiority and dependency. Augustine confirmed that while the male signified the mind, the female signified the body: "the concupiscential part, over which the mind bears rule."[52] For Aquinas, God created woman to help man, but even that role was qualified; woman, he maintained, was created by God "as a helper to man; not, indeed, as a helpmate in other works, as some say, since man can be more efficiently helped by another man in other works; but as a helper in the work of generation."[53] Within the divine hierarchy, most medieval theologians concluded, man was the beginning and end of woman, as God was the beginning and end of man.

———— ∾ ————

An even more damning view of women, and the justification for the Church's negative attitude toward them, resides in the story of Adam and Eve (Gen. 3 : 1–24). Eve's disregard of God's will, her capitulation to the serpent's enticement, her temptation of Adam, and their ultimate offense constituted, according to Catholic doctrine, the fall of humankind from God's grace. By their act of disobedience, the first parents were doomed to lives of suffering and anxiety. During the formative centuries of the new religion, Christian apologists identified Satan with the serpent and singled out Eve as the partner responsible for the Fall. Adam had succumbed to Eve's blandishments, but, as temptress, Eve received the larger share of the blame. Tertullian expressed the popular medieval view of women as the daughters of Eve:

> The sentence of God on this sex of yours lives on even in our times and so it is necessary that the guilt should live on, also. You are the one who opened the door to the Devil, you are the first who deserted the divine law; you are the one who persuaded him whom the Devil was not strong enough to attack. All too easily you destroyed the image of God, man. Because of your desert, that is, death, even the Son of God had to die. And you still think of putting adornments over . . . you?54

Like Paul, Tertullian believed that male and female were one in Jesus Christ and that, despite female subjection to male (Gen. 3 : 16), women would be redeemed equally with men. Nevertheless, as Tertullian pointed out, the Devil could not have lured Adam— the stronger partner—into sin, except through Eve. Weakness, self-indulgence, carnality, greed, and cunning were the primary iniquities ascribed to women by medieval misogynists, whose attitudes toward womankind ranged from active hostility to distrust and fear. Throughout the early Christian era, a vast literature expounded upon the threat that women presented to the moral and spiritual purity of men. These texts condemned women even as they attempted to constrain them. The Greek church father Clement of Alexandria advised that women cover their heads and faces with veils: "Women are not at all to be allowed to expose or lay bare any part of their bodies, lest both men and women fall: the one by being aroused to steal glances, the other by attracting the eyes of men to themselves."[55]

Women were excluded from roles of authority within the Church. They were forbidden to enter the priesthood or to touch the sacred vessels—though the belief that they threatened the ritual purity of Christianity seems to have crystallized only after the sixth century.[56] Not all early church fathers were as vitriolic as Tertullian in their condemnation of women. But even those who cultivated close spiritual friendships with women, such as Saint Jerome, encouraged women to renounce marriage.[57]

Officially, the Catholic church approved of matrimony as the means of procreation and the remedy for concupiscence. The early fathers often likened the union of man and woman to the marriage of Christ and the Church. Nevertheless, most theologians agreed that virgins were the prized portion of Christ's flock. Even medieval medical lore concurred, upholding the opinion that the urine of virgins, which was clear, bright, and thin, was superior to that of nonvirgins, which was dense, greasy, and cloudy.[58]

Prior to the fourteenth century, misogynic literature was primarily religious; but secular literature, too, such as the *dits* presented here, espoused the traditional church position regarding the female as inferior, as proved by the creation story, and sinful, as proved by the story of the Fall. The opening lines of the *Contenance* establish masculine primacy in God's plan, both in the assertion that men were "shaped in God's image" (2), and in the claim that they are the wiser of the two sexes (3). Only men, writes the author of the *Contenance,* have the capacity to "distinquish bad from good" (6). These lines recall Aquinas's assertion that woman is naturally subject to man, "because in man the discernment of reason predominates."[59] The final lines of the poem parallel the opening argument and link female inferiority with the Fall: "Que qui aime et croit fole fame / Gaste son temps, pert corps et ame" ("Who loves and trusts mad womankind / Damns soul and body, wastes his time," 175–76).

While the *Contenance* stresses woman's inferiority, the *Blasme* emphasizes her deceitfulness and subversiveness. The author of the *Blasme* makes pointed reference to spiritual death as the consequence of man's affection for woman: "Ki femme aime ou femme prise / Sovent en vient a gref juïse" ("Who loves or prizes womankind / Often ends up much maligned," 5–6). In an accusatory and rhetorical tone, he demands to know which of the two sexes bears primary responsibility for the initial disobedience to God (13) and for the exile from the Garden of Eden (14). Basic to the misogyny of the *Blasme* is the traditional opinion that the serpent chose to tempt Eve because she was deemed the weaker and more credulous of the first parents: "Pur ceo qe femme out fieble sens / L'enginnat primes li serpens; / Cil qui ne pout foul espleiter / Ad perempli per le mulier" ("Because of woman's weaker wit / She fell into the snake's gambit; / Her better half the lesser fool, / The snake used woman as his tool," 21–24). Eve's seduction of Adam consummated Satan's act of guile. To the medieval mind, woman and serpent were reciprocal images—one a metaphor for the other, and both symbolic of Satan. Slippery, cunning, and dangerous, the female herself was the serpent, cursed and condemned by God, like the snake in Genesis (3 : 14), to a lowly and servile existence. The parallel is driven home in the *Blasme;* "Ensi la fist a son semblant, / Sa fai lui tendi meintenant" ("The serpent made her in his image, / And she to him now renders homage," 31–32). Woman, he reiterates, is as venomous as a snake (70). The metaphor prevails in medieval literature and art, where women are often depicted with serpent/devils (figs. 12, 13).[60]

Eve's alleged depravity inspired much of the anti-female ha-

Fig. 12. Eve Holding the Serpent.
Reims Cathedral, 13th century.
Now in Paris, Musée des
Monuments français.

Fig. 13. The Devil Counseling Potiphar's Wife. Right Portal, North Porch, Chartres Cathedral, mid-13th century.

rangue of the *Blasme*. God's condemnation of Eve bequeaths, in the words of the *Blasme*, a "dowry" of childlishness, irrationality, pride, and jealousy (25–29). Woman has sown depravity since the beginning of time (33–34); poisonous and discordant (37–38), she is the root of all evil (39). Woman creates discord in marriage (37–38) and among friends (41–42); she appears devout but actually lacks humility (49–50); she fosters strife, war, and combat (53–60). The naming of evils descending from Eve was a popular medieval didactic device, utilized by medieval preachers such as Jacques de Vitry (d. 1240) and in medieval handbooks such as that of the Chevalier de la Tour Landry, who warns his daughters of Eve's "nine faults" that brought sin and death into the world.[61]

At the close of the *Blasme* the author dwells on specific examples of the inherently deceitful nature of woman as the scion of Eve. Woman easily surmounts and renounces shame and remorse (117–

18); she is "femme fole" against whom all men must be on their guard (123–24); like Satan, she is a creature who lies and betrays authority (100–06); she is dangerous to both body and soul: "Gardum nos cors de mal encumbrer; / Ne creez femme car ceo est lur mester, / Mentir, trahir, e gent enpoisoner" ("Let's keep our bodies safe from ill; / Don't believe her whose main devices / Are lies, betrayal, and toxic vices," 128–30).

One of the recurring themes in the anti-female topos is the threat presented by idle women. The freedom from responsibility enjoyed by the woman of the *Contenance* contributes to her volatility: "Or ne fait riens, ore ne fine; / Or tensera a sa voisine" ("Now she's idle, then can't sit tight; / Now with her neighbor picks a fight," 69–70). The *Blasme* emphasizes female mutability in a litany of contradictory attributes; she can be as gentle as a dove or a lamb (80–82) but as tough as a hedgehog (79) and as dominant as a falcon (81). Like the Devil, woman takes many shapes, all the more numerous because she enjoys excessive leisure time. The potential for evil among idle women preoccupied the authors of medieval handbooks of behavior; in the fourteenth century, Paolo de Certaldo warned husbands to ensure that their women be kept busy: "never allow them to be idle, for idleness is a great danger to both man and woman, but more to woman. . . ."[62]

In medieval times the position of women was often indicated by what they wore. Paul had admonished women to cover their heads when entering a church (presumably as a sign of humility and subordination), while men might leave their heads uncovered (1 Cor. 11 : 4–5). The apostle's directives are mentioned in the *Blasme* (17) where the author explains that women must wear head-coverings because of "la hunte de pecché, / Q'ele nous getta de notre fé" ("It is the sinner's shame / That drove us from our first domain," 19–20). The complaint that woman "monstera poitrine et col" ("bares her bosom, throat, and neck," *Contenance*, 80) is frequently heard in the sermons of medieval preachers familiar with the complaint of Clement of Alexandria that women, "lean their heads back . . . thereby exposing their throats with . . . such immodesty!"[63]

Women's outward appearance sometimes indicated their profession: municipal laws in many medieval French cities mandated that prostitutes should wear eye-catching items of clothing, such as red hoods, colored ribbons, and braids on their sleeves that contrasted with the colors of their costume. The prostitute's role as temptress and seducer was indeed embodied in the legislation even as her profession was gradually institutionalized.[64] Physical display, sexual seduction, and sin are linked in the *Contenance,* where the extended criticism of vanity and apparel precedes the author's conclusion that "fole fame," the prototypical Eve, will lead man to damnation (176). The same sentiment is expressed by Aquinas: self-adorning women are dangerous because they arouse lust, which constitutes a mortal sin.[65]

From New Testament epistles through the late medieval sermons, didactic writings warn against talkative women. According to Paul, women must not speak out in church or address the congregation (1 Cor. 14 : 34–35). In the later epistles, Timothy advises women to listen quietly, dress modestly, and do good deeds (1 Tim. 2 : 15). Silence was symbolic of the humility befitting the more servile of the sexes. The scolding wife, the gossip, and the chatterbox were vilified in the *fabliaux,* and dramatizations of the story of Noah, where Noah's wife was a stock figure of the prating, quarrelsome, and opinionated female, popularized that image. And in some French cities contentious and talkative women were shamed before church congregations by being made to wear heavy stones around their necks.[66] In the *Contenance* the author ascribes to woman disruptive and deceitful verbal behavior. She is shrill on occasion (60); she will rage at her maidservant (64), pick fights with her neighbors (70), and share confidences damaging to personal relations (73–74). Her "evil chatter," according to the *Blasme*, "sets friends against one another, / Turning brother against brother" (41–42). The Latin epilogue that follows the *Blasme* further reinforces the author's criticism of female chatter. Language is the tool woman uses to fulfill her role as the modern Eve; in the words of the *Blasme*, "Femme par sa douce parole, / Atret li home e puis l'afole" ("Her words are sweetness sugar-clad / To lure a man and drive him mad," 47–48). The evils of female verbosity and the damnation consequent to Eve's act of disobedience are vividly coupled in the line that compares woman to hell (95) and, by extension, to the all-receiving hell-mouth carved into stone exteriors of medieval churches and painted in the miniatures of countless manuscripts. Hollow and receptive, like the watering hole used in an earlier simile (89), the female hell-mouth is a vaginal image that signifies depravity and damnation. Resonant with sexuality, the image calls to mind the Old Testament proverb "A prostitute is a deep pit, a loose woman a narrow well" (Prov. 23 : 27).

As Eve provided the negative image of womankind, so the Virgin Mary, Mother of God and Queen of Heaven, provided the positive one. Eve had invoked damnation and death, but Mary, through Christ, blessed humankind with salvation and eternal life. Eve and Mary were complementary and contradictory moral counterparts, whose antithesis informed the ascriptive anti- and pro-female discourse of the Middle Ages. Though medieval woman was primarily associated with Eve, the image of Mary carried undeniably praiseworthy significance both as the paragon of religious virtue and as the ideal feminine type.[67]

Primary among Mary's positive characteristics was her freedom from carnality: not only was she conceived by divine intervention, but her own chastity was preserved by the immaculate conception of Jesus. Another of the Virgin's virtues was her status as Mother of God, and particularly her loving, suffering nature. In the eleventh century, Pope Gregory VII compared Mary to human mothers, claiming that she was "higher and better and more holy," and therefore "more gracious and tender toward every sinner."[68]

The equation of womankind and the Virgin Mary is basic to pro-female sentiment. At the beginning of the *Bien,* the author claims that no reasonable man will fail to honor women in the same way that he honors the blessed Virgin (11–14), thus equating Mary with womankind. He then points out that both the mightiest and the lowliest of men are born of woman (19–24), an obvious statement, but a reminder that (as maintained by early Church apologists), motherhood in and of itself was a positive aspect of womanhood. Timothy, for instance, wrote that women are saved through motherhood (1 Tim. 2:15). The thirteenth-century preacher Jacques de Vitry argued that God deliberately chose to have a woman as his mother. And in the fifteenth century, the notable medieval feminist Christine de Pizan argued that women's monopoly on motherhood brought them special distinction.[69]

Mary's importance as mediator in the quest for salvation received great emphasis during the thirteenth century. The exaltation of the Virgin culminated in the Marian cult that influenced the art, music, and literature of the high and late Middle Ages. Praise for Mary appears in the writings of the scholastics, as well as in the sermons of medieval preachers. The Dominican master-general Humbert de Romans observed that woman was not made from vile earth or from a servile part of her mate's body, but from his very respectable rib.[70] In the arts of the period Mary was frequently pictured enthroned, holding a book, the symbol of knowledge, or a scepter, the symbol of authority. She is the object of worship for commoners and queens (fig. 8). The author of the *Bien* regards women as moral agents when he writes, "Par fame destornez en iere" ("Woman educates the wayward," 48). Moreover, woman inculcates docility and gentleness ("Fame si fet simples et dous," 49), ideals traditionally fulfilled by the Mother of God.

The new emphasis on the miracle-working powers of the Virgin reflected in the literature and art of the thirteenth century may have inspired the claim in the *Bien* that "Fame si fet tant de merveilles / Que la moitié n'en conteroie" ("Women work so many marvels / That I could only tell you half," 80–81). Mary's elevation to a prestigious and authoritative role is best represented by her status as Bride of Christ and Queen of Heaven. On the carved stone portals of many thirteenth-century churches (themselves dedicated to Notre-Dame—Our Lady), and in illuminated manuscripts, Mary is pictured as coequal with Christ, sharing his throne as rule of heaven, wearing royal robes, and receiving the crown of heaven from him or from attendant angels (fig. 14).[71] Medieval literature also carries this message of triumph. For instance, in his widely acclaimed sermon *Ad omnes mulieres,* Humbert de Romans compares womankind to the Virgin Mary, whom Christ has set above the angels within the heavenly court.[72] The phrasing in the *Bien* (15–16) is almost identical.

When the author of the *Bien* states that eminent men hold women in high acclaim (25–28), he reminds his listeners that those who praise women are in good company. Indeed, historical evidence supports his thesis. In the late eleventh century, Marbode, bishop of Rennes, wrote a series of poems on the *mulier bona* or good wife, honoring women as cooks, housekeepers, and nurturers, and pointing out the crucial role that women played in maintaining domestic order. Historically, women held a major place in family life. Since women were usually at least ten years younger than their husbands, they often interceded between fathers and children, to whom they were closer in age.[73] As intermediaries between generations, women might mirror Mary's role as intercessor, thus earning

Fig. 14. Coronation of the Virgin. Central Portal, North Porch, Chartres Cathedral, mid-13th century.

prestige and influence within the household. Among aristocrats, the literature of courtly love inspired a positive shift in attitudes toward women.[74] The influential preacher Jacques de Vitry attributed his success to the guidance and prayers of Marie of Oignies, the mother of the female religious group known as the Béguines.[75] Around 1300 the French scholar Pierre de Blois wrote a treatise praising the civilizing powers of women and advocating that clever women be educated as medical missionaries.[76] And in the early fourteenth century, the radical theologian William of Occam argued that women should be included on church councils.[77] Compared with these avant-garde thinkers, the author of the *Bien* seems conservative indeed. His views approximate those of the thirteenth-century churchman Hermann of Steinfeld who, regarding the Virgin as his companion and source of solace, condemned his fellow clerics for demeaning women.[78]

The Mother of God—prototype of the best in women—is the image that shaped the pro-female language of the *Bien.* Nevertheless, between the Virgin Mary and flesh-and-blood medieval women the gap was wide. In the *Bien,* as in most literature of this period, Mary remains isolated from the human dimension of everyday women who raised children, cooked meals, washed clothes, and performed numerous other household tasks totally ignored in the *Bien.* Still, the author did recognize that womankind should not be demeaned, if for no other reason than, as Luke reports (10 : 38–42), Jesus himself regarded the female sex favorably: "Je ne sai clerc, ne lai, ne prestre / Que de fame puist consirrer, / Se il ne veut trop meserrer / Envers Dieu en mainte maniere" ("Neither cleric, priest, nor layman / Can from women turn away, / If he does not wish to stray / Sinfully from the good Lord," 44–47). To abandon womankind, argues the author, is unchristian.

At the same time that medieval educators were reassessing women more favorably, or more precisely, revising their position in terms of a glorified image of the Virgin Mary, society was imposing on women a new round of constraints. Thirteenth-century religious orders sought to limit female membership in their branches, religious women were increasingly separated from men, and the practice of cloistering women was more strictly enforced.[79] Various factors contributed to these impositions, including the growing number of husbandless women (especially in urban communities), the ensuing proliferation of monastic houses for women, and the expanding influence of women in popular literature and life. Women mystics pervaded the thirteenth-century religious scene, their ecstasies recorded in vernacular poetry brimming with vivid visions of Christ and the Virgin. Some, like the followers of Guglielma of Milan (d. 1279), who claimed to be the female incarnation of the Holy Spirit, sought to establish a new church led by women.[80] The "flowering of female piety"[81] included the birth of unsanctioned religious groups such as the Béguines, who set themselves apart from the world and pursued lives of meditation, manual labor, and worship. An essentially urban phenomenon, the Béguines were condemned for heterodoxy in 1311. Heretical societies attracted women of all classes and presented a threat to both male authority and church doctrine. Persecution was inevitable.[82]

At the end of the thirteenth century, the legal system reinforced restrictive attitudes toward women. In order to preserve male dominance of labor, new laws denied women entry into certain trades. In regions of northern France the influence of Roman law, which supported the role of monarchs and centralism in general, contributed to the more precise definition of landholding rights and position. Roman law also strengthened the power of the male head of the household over his family and retainers. The overall result was an increasingly authoritative concept of the French kingdom as a patriarchal community.[83] Though the *Contenance* and the *Blasme* belong to a long misogynic literary tradition, the *Blasme,* already in circulation before 1280, surely voices the hostility of this patriarchy.[84]

———————

In reviewing the *dits* in their historical context, some final observations may be made. For instance, while the poems say a great deal about women, they evidence little regard for women as wives. Thirteenth- and fourteenth-century marriage manuals offer positive assessments of the carnal and spiritual union of man and woman.[85] Yet nowhere in these three poems, not even in the *Bien,* is woman appraised as a marriage partner. The idea of *amisté,* or

loving friendship between man and woman, which informs medi-
eval marriage treatises, is never mentioned. References to marriage
appear only in the Latin verse that concludes the *Blasme,* where the
author laments that since his marriage his life has been disjointed
and calamitous,[86] and in the poem itself, where the author remarks
that in taking a husband woman robs his family (43–44). Although
the *Blasme* expresses antimatrimonial sentiment, the other two *dits*
ignore the subject of marriage entirely.

It is also worth considering that among our "three medieval
views of women" a rather wide variety of subtle affective responses
to women emerges. The male voice in the *Contenance* is paternal
and personal. With regard to womankind, the author opines that
what makes one laugh may make another cry (173) but that in
general women are a fickle breed (163) who take men's breath
away (79), waste their time (176), and, at worst, lead them to death
and damnation (176). Nevertheless the poet sketches the habits of a
woman in fine detail: she spreads out her jewels and gazes at them
(103–04), flutters like a moulting bird (44), gets the blues and
weeps (30–31), winks and flirts (146–47), and behaves like an
attentive and flattering paramour (148–49). Such specific observa-
tions ring true and contrast with the more generalized and stereo-
typed imagery of the other two poems. The keenness of the author's
observations suggests that he has looked closely at women, and not
without some enjoyment.

On the other hand, the praise sung in the *Bien* rings rather
hollow. An impersonal eulogy at best, it evinces no deep affection
for women, nor any admiration derived from firsthand experience
with the female sex. If the author has enjoyed a female friend or
lover or has benefited from female nurturing he does not record
those experiences here. He simply honors women for their kinship
with the Virgin, for their biological role as mothers, and for their
"many marvels" (80), the particulars of which he does not enumer-

ate, for the brevity of the poem itself (it is the shortest of the three) suggests that he has not been able to come up with a very long list. The Virgin Mary is indeed the foil—the model of perfection—against which the imperfections of flesh-and-blood females show up more distinctly. Finally, it is the public rather than the private woman that the author of the *Bien* extols. Not surprisingly, he perceives feminine virtues mainly in terms of woman's relationship to man. He enumerates the ways in which man benefits from the existence of woman rather than praising her as a creature in her own right.

In the *Blasme* the affective response to women is clearly one of fear. The author emphasizes the intrinsic sinfulness of womankind and presents an ascriptive catalogue of specific dangers: women give bad advice (98), abandon and betray their lovers (104), rob and slander (110–11), among other disreputable deeds. Potentially at the mercy of women, men must maintain their guard. Embedded in this defensive attitude that lies at the heart of most misogynic literature is the implicit assertion—so graphically conveyed in the animal/woman comparisons of lines 69–87—that women are keen, clever, and capable of outsmarting men. Women's superior guile and cunning are seen as dangerous native endowments.

The authors of the *Contenance* and the *Blasme* assume a prophetic posture, warning their comrades of the dangers of womankind and tendering their frank advice in a tone of mock confidentiality. We might regard the basically defensive cast of these poems as intrinsic to the eternal battle of the sexes founded in the fact of heterogeneity, or we could see in such satiric abuse a reaction to historic developments that were giving women more opportunities to challenge male dominance in various social and economic spheres. In either case, the three poems presented here indisputably reflect a tension that is uncomfortably familiar even in our own time.

Taken as a unit, these poems convey the deep ambivalence of medieval men toward women. The Eve/Mary dualism permitted woman to hold a high place in the scheme of Christian redemption yet at the same time bear primary responsibility for sin and corruption. This dualism was a major source of conflicting attitudes toward medieval women; but more complex types of ambivalence existed as well. Men sought different kinds of satisfaction from mothers, wives, and whores. Did they not also love and fear each of these female types in different ways? Surely, as our poems demonstrate, medieval man viewed woman as both desirable and dangerous, and also as essentially "opposite" or different. By assessing the opposite sex and isolating its vices and virtues, men endeavored to assert their superiority. There is no single image of medieval woman presented in these poems, nor any unanimous response to her presence in medieval society. But that her existence in a man's world provided both danger and delight, as well as a foil for male self-distinction, is unquestionable.

Notes

For a comprehensive bibliography on medieval women, see Frey et al. 1982.

   1. For historical background, see Chédeville et al. 1980: 186–323; Fawtier 1962: 27–47; Hallam 1980: 257–324; Langlois 1969: 353–79; Mundy and Riesenberg 1958: 26–56; Strayer 1980; and Thrupp 1964. On the debate as to whether thirteenth-century Paris held a population of 80,000 or 240,000, see Hallam 1980: 286–88 and Herlihy 1984: 136–48.
   2. Mundy 1982: 237. I am grateful to Patricia Humphrey for bringing this essay to my attention. On the social origins of courtly poets, see Zumthor 1972: 31–44, 64–82. The problem of making class distinctions in the late Capetian era is complicated by marriage alliances between members of the middle class and feudal aristocrats (see Bloch 1977: 227 and Pegues 1962: 216).

3. On the subject of male and female "voices" in medieval poetry, see Plummer 1981.

4. Medieval inheritance practices are characterized by regional, demographic, and class differences. Among Norman non-noble families, for instance, an equal division of property among heirs was the rule; see Yver 1966: 90–107. On French matrimonial laws and inheritance customs in general, see Bloch 1966: 200–08; Gold 1985: 116–52; Hadju 1980: 122–44; O'Faolain and Martines 1973: 148–51; Shahar 1983: 81–88, 126–31; and Gies 1987: 128–29, 186–91, who also describes inheritance practices among artisans, 149–51.

5. Duby 1977: 116–22; McNamara and Wemple 1977: 111–12. On the "debasement" of the feudal relationship from the twelfth century on, see Strayer 1971: 77–89.

6. For evidence of women playing a more direct role in the management of their own property, see Casey 1976: 233–34; Gies 1987: 182–83, 195; and Hadju 1980: 127, 139–40. Women began using their own seals on legal documents during this period (see Rezak 1985: xi and her longer study in Erler and Kowaleski 1988: 61–82). On powerful noblewomen, especially widows, see Labarge 1987: 80–94, 166–67 and Gies 1978: 97–142. For a comparative view of late medieval rural Englishwomen, property and household responsibilities, see Hanawalt 1986: 140–55.

7. Labarge 1987: 32; Kirshner 1985: 256–303; Shahar 1983: 11–21. On the freedom to select mates, see Donahue 8 (1983): 144–58; Noonan 1973: 419–34; and Sheehan 1978: 4–15. On wife-beating, see Gies 1987: 181; Labarge 1987: 26, 204; and O'Faolain and Martines 1973: 175.

8. Herlihy 1985: 104–07. On the relationship between ages at marriage and inheritance, see Gies 1987: 141–45, 184.

9. In northern France between 1100 and 1300, wives survived husbands 64.2 percent of the time, Hadju 1980: 129. For demographic estimates, see Duby 1964 and Herlihy 1984: 145. In England the average life expectancy of women was thirty-one to thirty-three years as compared with twenty-one to twenty-four years for men, 46 percent of whom died in combat while still in their teens, Shahar 1983: 129. See also Labarge 1987: 21–24.

10. Gold 1985: 130–34; Hadju 1980: 129–31; Shahar 1983: 93–98.

11. Power 1975: 76–88; Shahar 1983: 154–65.

12. Bornstein 1983: 33–34, 59–60; Labarge 1987: 38–39.

13. O'Faolain and Martines 1973: 167, 169. But compare the opinion of the Knight de la Tour Landry, who favored women's reading edifying literature (La Tour Landry n.d.: xxii, 171); and Francesco Barberino, whose early fourteenth-century courtesy book urged women, especially those who might inherit property, to learn to read and write (Bell 1982: 755–56, republished in Erler and Kowaleski 1988: 149–87. I am indebted to JoAnn McNamara for this reference).

14. Gies 1978: 63–76; Power 1975: 89–99; Herlihy 1985: 13; Labarge 1987: 10, 98–110. Convents were closed to peasant women, who, in lieu of marriage, usually became servants and laborers; Gies 1987: 169.

15. Andreas 1941: 31. Considerable scholarly controversy exists over the meaning and influence of Andreas's so-called code of courtly love.

16. Quoted in Dronke 1984: 92. On women and musical entertainment, see Rokseth 1935: 464–80 and Labarge 1987: 464–80.

17. Lehmann 1952: 418; Lucas 1983: 172–73. On medieval women as literary patrons, see Bell 1982: 750, 759–60; Holzknecht 1966: 44–45, 90–115, 218–19; McCash [in press]. On women's charitable donations, see Berman 1985: 53–68 and Labarge 1987: 85–92.

18. Boileau 1879. On the presence of women in the medieval guilds, see Casey 1976: 224–29; Labarge 1987: 150–56, 226–31; Lehmann 1952: 429–76; O'Faolain and Martines 1973: 158; and Shahar 1983: 190–98.

19. Labarge 1987: 152. On usury in Toulouse, see Mundy 1982: 233.

20. Shahar 1987: 198. On urban women's rights, see Hadju 1980: 130 and Power 1975: 9–12.

21. Ibid., 67; Bornstein 1983: 65, 96; Labarge 1987: 153, 163. The *cervoisers* (brewers) granted the title of master only to widows, Lehmann 1952: 457.

22. Bullough and Brundage 1982: 149–60, 176–86; Labarge 1987: 195–204; Markun 1962: 56–63; Otis 1985: 25–31; Rossiaud 1988: 44–45, 124–25; and Shahar 1983: 206–08.

23. Particularly fascinating is the case brought against Jacoba Felicie in the court of Paris in 1322 (discussed in Hughes 1943: 82–86 and Labarge 1987: 175–78). Cures practiced by elderly women were often associated with witchcraft, Hughes 1943: 93–99. On medieval women and medicine,

see also Bornstein 1983: 99; Jacquart 1981: 47–55; Lehmann 1952: 71–76; Lemay 1985: 17–36; and Labarge 1987: 11–12, 169–94. On the term *miresse* (feminine form of *mire*), see Jacquart 1981: 37–38, 54.

24. Lehmann 1952: 443. The percentage of women among the total number of individuals subject to taxes remains relatively steady, however; see Labarge 1987: 151.

25. See Hanawalt 1976: 125, 133, whose conclusions are based on an examination of English gaol delivery rolls. On women and the medieval courts, see also Shahar 1983: 81–93, 210–12; and Labarge 1987: 154–56, 163–64, 204–10. On infanticide and its penalties in various parts of France, see Brissaud 1972: 243–48 and Kellum 1974: 367–88.

26. Apparently, it was feared that corpses left on the gallows might be profaned; see Labarge 1987: 206 and Shahar 1983: 20–21.

27. La Tour Landry n.d.: 329–33.

28. McNeill and Gamer 1938: 209. Such tradition, which goes back to biblical times, was also a practical measure for determining the paternity of a child *in utero*.

29. Bornstein 1983: 74.

30. Chédeville et al. 1980: 324–47; Howell 1987: 27–46, 174–83; Mundy and Riesenberg 1958: 66–90. On the *fabliau* in relation to town life, see Cooke: 1974 and 1976; Ménard 1983; and Nykrog 1957.

31. Pike 1938: 356.

32. Andreas 1941: 200. For examples of women's cunning as described in thirteenth-century sermon literature, see Crane 1890: 95–96, 112.

33. Bornstein 1983: 40–42; also 37–38, 53–54, and 59–60.

34. Evans 1952: 21.

35. Kraemer 1920: 10–36; Greenfield 1918: 107.

36. Sronkova 1954: 31.

37. Evans 1952: 14–15. For similar legislation in Montpellier, see Kraemer 1920: 36.

38. Duplès-Agier 1854: 176–81.

39. La Tour Landry n.d.: 54.

40. Evans 1952: 24–25. Compare Jean de Venette's slightly later complaints of extravagance in male and female costume in Newhall 1953: 34, 62–63.

41. Gies 1978: 39.

42. Evans 1952: 18; compare Vincent 1935: 44.

43. The wide variety of terms used for late medieval headgear makes it difficult to identify their precise meaning. Such is the case with *"nasiere"* (*Contenance,* 117), which may describe a type of mask. Municipal ordinances forbade women to wear masks in public, Greenfield 1918: 119; see also Coulton 1907: 220.

44. In the late thirteenth century, Jean de Meun, the author of the second part of the *Roman de la Rose,* compared the "horns" to those of rams, snails, and unicorns (see Evans 1952: 24); but affectations in headgear—both men and women's—were only in their infancy in Jean's time. The following decades ushered in more dramatic and outrageous types of head-coverings. For these novelties, the French blamed the English, but most of Europe looked to France for leadership in fashion (see Scott 1980: 57 and Sronkova 1954: 38).

45. Tertullian 1959: 138.

46. Ibid., 135–36. The phrase describing makeup as "the devil's soap" appears in Old English sermon literature, Morris 1973: 52–53. For an example from the sermons of the thirteenth-century Guibertus de Tornaco, see d'Avray and Tausche 1980: 102.

47. Evans 1952: 29–31 and Houston 1979: passim. For an extensive bibliography on late medieval costume, see Piponnier 1970: 367–72.

48. Andreas 1941: 204.

49. Aristotle 1953: 728–30, 732, 737, 766. See also Bullough 1973: 487–93 and Horowitz 1976: 183–213.

50. Lemay 1978: 395.

51. Aquinas 1947: I, 466. For a summary of Aquinas's views on women, see Ferrante 1975: 101–05.

52. Augustine 1887: 524.

53. Aquinas 1947: I, 466.

54. Tertullian 1959: 118.

55. Clement of Alexandria 1954: 123; also 187–88.

56. Wemple 1981: 135–39. See also McNamara 1983 and Parvey 1974: 117–49.

57. Jerome's letters, which describe the physically and spiritually polluting nature of sex, have been viewed as "the by-product of violent libidinal repression" by Ruether 1979: 169–70. On virginity as a medieval ideal, see Bugge 1975: passim.

58. O'Faolain and Martines 1973: 142. On praise of virginity over marriage in medieval courtesy books, see Bornstein 1983: 21–25; in vernacular and Latin sermons, see Roberts 1985: 103–18.

59. Aquinas 1947: I, 466.

60. Kraus 1982: 79–98.

61. La Tour Landry n.d.: 77–85. According to Jacques de Vitry, the Devil begat nine daughters and married them to various classes of men: Simony to the clergy, Hypocrisy to monks, Rapine to soldiers, Usury to the *bourgeoisie*, Knavery to merchants, Sacrilege to farmers who refused to pay tithes, Dishonest Service to laborers, Rich and Unnecessary Clothing to women, and Lust to all men (in Crane 1890: 101, 235–36).

62. Quoted in O'Faolain and Martines 1973: 169.

63. Clement of Alexandria 1954: 122. See also Caird 1971: 268–81.

64. Bullough and Brundage 1982: 182; Labarge 1987: 198–200; Markun 1922: 60; Otis 1985: 100–10; Rossiaud 1988: 55–85; and Shahar 1983: 209.

65. Aquinas 1947: II, 1883.

66. Labarge 1987: 205. See also Coulton 1907: 28–29.

67. Warner 1976: xxiv, 50–67; Purtle 1982: 3–15; and Ruether 1977: passim.

68. Quoted in Gold 1985: 70. On virgin birth and immaculate conception, see Bugge 1975: 141–54.

69. Christine 1982: 218. Jacques de Vitry's words are: "... deus voluit habere feminam matrem, et non hominem patrem," quoted in d'Avray and Tausche 1980: 107.

70. Brett 1984: 68. On the use of the "rib-*topos*" in sermon literature, see d'Avray and Tausche 1980: 106.

71. Verdier 1980: passim; Gold 1985: 61–68. On the *sponsa Christi* motif, see Bugge 1975: 90–96 and Purtle 1982: 98–126.

72. "Also no pure man will be above the angels ... as will a pure

woman . . . and this will be in the person of the Blessed Virgin"; quoted in Brett 1984: 68. One-fifth of Herman's sermons are devoted to women, including one dedicated to prostitutes.

73. Herlihy 1985: 116, 121, 129.

74. On the other hand, some view courtly love as fundamentally misogynic; see Duby 1978: 108.

75. Labarge 1985: 116–17.

76. Hughes 1943: 137–38; see also Jarrett 1926: 92–93.

77. Shahar 1983: 259.

78. Herlihy 1985: 119–20.

79. In 1299 Pope Boniface VIII issued an edict making the enclosure of nuns binding on all religious orders; see Lucas 1983: 52–53 and McLaughlin 1974: 242–43.

80. So vocal were these women that Pope Boniface VIII finally condemned all women "who taught new dogma and led immoral lives"; Wessley 1978: 291.

81. Bynum 1982: 71; Bolton 1976: 141–65; McLaughlin 1980: 99–130. Bynum interprets the mysticism of thirteenth-century women as "an alternative to the authority of [clerical] office" (261), but the adherence of women to heretical sects has also been ascribed to their search for economic security (Wessley 1978: 299–300). On recluses and mystics, see Labarge 1987: 129–42.

82. A case in point is that of Marguerite Porete, a mystic and Béguine whose vernacular meditations on the soul's capacity to unite with God were condemned as heretical; Marguerite was burned in Paris in 1310. See Bryant 1984: 203–26; Coulton 1907: 201; Dronke 1984: 217–28; and Petroff 1986: 280–83, 294–98. For a brief account of the Béguines, see Labarge 1987: 115–20.

83. The "progrès du droit romain" contributed to "une transformation dans les mentalités juridiques qui joue contre la femme"; in Payen 1977: 430; also see Donahue 1983: 151–56; Hadju 1980: 122–29; Hallam 1980: 263; Howell 1987: 181–83; Mundy and Riesenberg 1958: 59, 90; and Shahar 1983: 171.

84. Compare the second part of the *Roman de la Rose*, composed by

Jean de Meun around 1275, which also denounces womankind and condemns courtly conventions as false and deceptive.

85. Parmisano 1969: 606. For sermon literature, see Crane 1890: 99–100 and d'Avray and Tausche 1980: 87–88, 114–17.

86. For similar medieval diatribes against marriage, see John of Salisbury in Pike 1938: 354–61; *De coniuge non ducenda* (ca. 1225–50) in Rigg 1986; and Matheolus's antimatrimonial "complaint" (ca. 1290–91), in Matheolus 1892–1905. For examples of quarrelsome and contrary wives in sermon *exempla*, see Jacques de Vitry in Crane 1890: 98–99.

La Contenance
des Fames

La Contenance
des Fames

Se homs congnoissoit l'avantage
Que Dieux quant le fist a s'ymage
Li donna—ce fu congnoissance—
Moult auroit au cuer grant poissance
Quant d'en usier ne sauroit rien   5
A decevrier le mal du bien.
Cilz a congnoissance perdue
Qui du bien au mal se remue,
Et met cuer et cors et avoir
En lieu dont ne le puet revoir;   10
Et de franchise entre en servage
Et son corps gaste en fol usage
Et met sa pensee et sa cure
En feme, qui a petit cure
Comment aucune chose avieingne   15
Mais qu'a son vouloir se contieingne.
Si vous en diray la semblance,
La maniere et la contenence;
Et ne le tieingne nul a fable:
Moult a feme le cuer muable,   20
Et tressaillant et dur et tendre,
Si qu'a pou veult a bien entendre

The Ways
of Women

If men understood the advantage
Of having been shaped in God's image,*
With reason for their dower,
Their hearts would swell with power
When they used it as they should   5
To distinguish bad from good.*
He surely has lost his mind*
Who would good in evil find,
Who invests heart, body, and gain
Where they cannot be reclaimed;   10
Over freedom chooses slavery,
Wastes his body in debauchery,
Investing heart and mind
In frivolous womankind,
Who doesn't care a jot   15
For things that suit her not.*
My poem to you conveys
Female manners, female ways;
And let none deem disputable*
That a woman's heart is mutable,*   20
Fluttering from tender to cold,
She will never be cajoled,

Fors tant coume son cuer li donne.
Or le toult, ore l'abandonne,
Or le donne, or le retrait,   *25*
Ce qu'elle puet a li attrait.
Feme a un cuer par heritage
Qui ne puet estre en un estage.
Or s'esjouist, or se conforte;
Or reva, or se desconforte;   *30*
Or semble qu'el soit couroucee;
Or est pensive, or est lee;
Or est viguereuse, or est vaine;
Or est malade, or est saine;
Or se siet, or ne se veult seoir;   *35*
Or ne veult nul hom veoir;
Or le veult, or ne le veult mie;
Or se lie, or se gravie.
Or fait semblant qu'elle est estable,
Orendroit sera delitable.   *40*
Or est simple, puis orgueilleuse;
Or diligent, or pereceuse;
Or ne se muet, or se remue;
Or se tient com oisel en mue;
Or est douce, or est amere;   *45*
Or est marrastre, or est mere.
Or ne li chaut que elle face;
Or veult avoir de touz la grace.
Or se contient moult sagement,
Or plainement, or baudeement.   *50*
Or est sauvage, or est privee;
Ore veult paiz, or veult meslee.
Or ne dit mot, et ore parle;
Or requiert l'ombre, puis le hale.

Except as her heart inclines.
Now she wants it, now declines,*
Now she'll give, then she'll retrieve   25
As fancy moves her to conceive.
A woman's heart is just not able
To chart a course that's firm or stable.*
Now she's merry, her spirits soar;
Now she dreams, she's blue once more;   30
Now it seems that she is wrathful;
Now she's pensive, now she's cheerful;
Now she's strong, and now she's weak;
Now she's ill, then at her peak;
Now she sits, now wants to stand;   35
Now she won't see any man;
Now she craves some, now wants none;
Now she's gay, then she's no fun;*
Now assumes a steadfast calm;*
Now suddenly she's full of charm;   40
Now unpretentious, now full of pride;
Now works hard, then lets all slide;
Now she's still, then stirs and putters;
Just like a moulting bird she flutters;*
Now she's gentle, now she's tart;   45
Cruel stepmother, mother sweet of heart;*
Now she cares not what she's doing;
Now she seeks the whole world's wooing;
Now she's proper as a crumpet;*
Now unrestrained, indeed, a strumpet;   50
Now she's wild, now she's demure;
Now wants peace, then starts a war;*
Now says nothing, now chatters on;
Retires in shade, then wants the sun;*

Or veult repos, or veult labour;   55
Or queurt au moulin, puis au four;
Or vient, or reva en la hale;
Or queurt a l'uis, puis en la sale.
Or veult froit, ore veult chaut;
Ore conseille, or parle haut.   60
Orendroit veult estre louee;
De riens ne veult estre blamee.
Orendroit fera belle chiere;
Puis se prent a sa chamberiere
Dont aucune foiz est jalouse.   65
Orendroit sera enviouse
De sa voisine qui aura
Plus beaux jouyaux qu'elle n'aura.
Or ne fait riens, ore ne fine;
Or tensera a sa voisine.   70
Souvent ira chez sa commere—
Ore la het, ore la chiere,
Or li dira, "Tel clerc me prie"
(Et celle est de l'autre amie).
Et pour dire plus de merveilles   75
Yra aux vespres et aus veilles,
Au sermon, en pelerinage.
Or fait le humble, puis le sage.
(Qui plus l'esgarde plus est fol!)
Or monstrera poitrine et col   80
Or est liee, or est cornue,
Or se va monstrier par la rue.
A soy sera d'aucun complainte,
Or se fait moult juste et moult sainte.
Ce que fait l'une, ne fait l'autre;   85
L'une veult d'un, l'autre veult d'autre.

Now wants to rest, now wants to labor;   55
Runs to the mill, then to a neighbor;*
Then to and fro and down the hall;
From room to room, she fills them all;*
Now she's warm, then has a chill;
Now she whispers,* then she's shrill.   60
Now your praises will she claim;
For nothing will she take the blame;
Now she's pleasant and she's cheerful;
Now she gives her maid* an earful,
Since the wench has fired her envy.   65
Now she burns with jealousy
Of her ladyfriend* who dresses
In finer jewels than she possesses.
Now she's idle, then can't sit tight;*
Now with her neighbor picks a fight.*   70
Often to her crony flies—
Whom now she'll love and now despise,
Confides, "That fellow woos me"
To the one who keeps him company.*
And then, more wondrous thing to say   75
She goes to church both night and day*
To sermons and on pilgrimage.*
Now she's humble, then she's sage.
(Who studies women becomes a wreck!)*
She bares her bosom, throat, and neck;   80
She binds her hair (horn-shapes will do)*
And shows off on the avenue.
She will not tolerate complaint,
She's lady justice and a saint.
What one woman does, another won't: 85
If one wants something, the other won't.

A dedire aucune besoingne,
Ne li convient ja querre essoingne,
Ja de parlier ne cessera;
Ce que feme pense, fera,   90
Soit bon, soit mal s'elle onques puet.
Et li chastïer pas n'estuet
Cilz se travaille, que qu'en die,
Et je le tieng a grant foulie
Car a ce faire riens ne vaut.   95
Or a le cuer coy, or l'a baut;
Ore n'est mie a son gré;
Ore remonte le degré;
Or entrera dedans sa chambre;
Ore veult may, or veult septembre;   100
Or envie escrin, or envie huche,
Orendroit poire ou pome succe;
Ses jouyaux prent, si le[s] remire—
Or les desploie, or les atire.
Or s'estent, or souspire, or geint;   105
Or s'esvertue, or se faint.
Or queurt a destre, or a senestre;
Et ore fuit a la fenestre.
Or chante, or pense, or rit, or pleure;
Moult mue son cuer en pou de heure!   110
Or est un pou descoulouree;
Ore sera toute fardee;
Or est sanz fart, or est sanz painte,
Chascun jour en maniere mainte
Ore se coife, or se lie;   115
Or se descoife, or se deslie.
Or a musel, or a nasiere,
Or a frontel, or a baniere,

Why bother to contradict her?
Pure logic won't restrict her.*
She'll talk your head off,
Do whatever she thinks of,   90
Whether good or bad or wise;*
It is useless to chastise,
And he who even tries*
Plays the fool in my eyes.
For the task is profitless.   95
Her heart's at peace and then it's restless;*
Now there's nothing suits her taste;
Now it's upstairs, off in haste;
To her room she flies away;
Prays for September, then for May;   100
Now wants a jewelbox, now a chest for storing,*
An apple or a pear for gnawing.*
She takes her jewels out for display—
Spreads them out, hides them away.
Now she stretches, sighs, then moans;   105
Now energetic, then lazybones.
Now rushes left, then rushes right;*
Now to the window she takes flight.
Now sings, now thinks, now laughs, now cries;*
Her mood will change, just blink your eyes!*   110
Now her face is wan and faint;
Now she's masked with makeup paint;
Now takes off the rouge and clay.*
She dons a new face every day.
Now she coifs, her hair she binds;   115
Now uncoifs, and now unbinds.*
Now she masks, now veils her face,*
Headband or kerchief sets in place,

Or a chapel, or a couronne,
Orendroit sa face abandonne   *120*
A veoir, et puis la requeuvre.
(C'est merveille que de leur euvre!)
Or est lavee, or est pignee,
Or est coifee, or est trecee.
Et moult tendroit a grant desdaing   *125*
S'elle n'avoit souvent le baing.
Or va a l'uis, si se regarde
Se nesun de li se prent garde.
Son mantel par devant desploie
Pour ce qu'on voie la courroie.   *130*
S'el n'a mantel, lieve le bout
De son sourcot, qu'on voie soubt
S'elle a bonne cote ou pelice.
Et moult se tendroit fole et nice
S'el n'est appareillee a droit.   *135*
Et s'el ne l'est tout orendroit,
Deffait et refait de rechief;
Or ratournera son chief
De guimple, de son chapellot.
Moult li envie quant elle ot   *140*
Qu'autre soit mieux appareillee.
Mais qui la voudroit faire liee,
Si li die que on la tient
Celle qui plus bel se maintient.
Or se mire, or se coloie,   *145*
Or fait le mignot, or le coie.
Or guigne, or redrece l'uel;
Or resera de bel acuel.
Orendroit sera moult escoute—
Nus ne vous porroit dire toute   *150*

Now a cap, now a crown,
Uncovered, see her face and brow,   120
The next day it is veiled again.
(Such marvels clearly take much pain!)
Now she's washed and combed her hair,
Now she's brushed and braided there.
She would surely find it scathing,   125
To forgo her frequent bathing.
She will go stand at her door
To make sure she's not ignored.
She'll open her mantle* wide
To reveal the belt inside,   130
Or lift surcoat* to show
What adorns her frame below:
Her good dress or fur-trimmed gown.*
She would never live it down*
To be dressed improperly.   135
If she's not, then instantly
She will strip and start again,
From her toes up to her chin,*
Fix her wimple or her bonnet.*
She will brood and grieve upon it   140
If another dresses better.
If one wishes to delight her,
Let him say that she is found
The most beautiful lady around.
Now she flutters in the glass,*   145
A coquette, a demure lass.
Now she winks, then lowers her eyes;*
She'll entice and patronize.
Attentive as a well-trained dog—
No one could ever catalogue   150

Leur maniere ne leur afaire.
Tant y a feme scet bon taire
Ce que l'en li dit et conseille.
Or remet sa main a s'oreille
Pour sa cornete redrecier;   *155*
Or veult faire, puis depecier,
Or se refait appareillier.
Or veult dormir, or veult veillier;
Or changera seurcot ou cote.
"Huche Alison! Huche Marote!"   *160*
Moult souvent mue contenance,
Or ne veult jeu, or ne veult dance;
Or va avant, or va arriere;
En tel guise et en tel maniere—
Souvent les dames se demainent,   *165*
Qui moult d'elle cointir se painent.
D'autres manieres ont en eulz
Qu'autre foiz, se j'estoie oiseux,
Et vous tout a loisir trouvoie,
Clerement le deviseroie.   *170*
Mais touz voirz ne sont bons a dire.
Dont l'une plaint, l'autre veult rire.
A vaine foiz l'ay je veü
Mais tant vous di qu'ay congneü:
Que qui aime et croit fole fame   *175*
Gaste son temps, pert corps et ame.

The ways of females old and young.*
When it comes to women, men, hold your tongue!
Advice, don't even volunteer:
She'll put her hand up to her ear,
But only to adjust her cap,*   155
To set it right, then to unwrap
And then redo it as before.
Now she'll wake, now sleep some more;
Now she'll change her dress or coat,
"Quick, Alison! Come here, Marote!"*   160
Her moods will all too often vary:
For games and dances she won't tarry;
Now she proceeds, now retreats,
Such are their follies and their feats—*
Often women carry on,   165
Take great pains to self-adorn!
More female foibles would I share
If I but had the time to spare,
And if you had the hours and strength,
I'd spin my tales at greater length;   170
Into all truths one cannot pry;*
What makes one laugh, makes another cry.
But I have seen enough to know
And this I say, I know it's so:
Who loves and trusts mad womankind   175
Damns soul and body, wastes his time.*

Variants

La Contenance des Fames

B = Besançon; D = Dijon; P = Paris 1593; R = Paris 12483

Lines

4	*R: missing line*
9	*B:* Et met son terre . . . ; *P: missing line*
10	*P: missing line*
12	*BPR:* Et son temps gaste . . .
21	*R:* Mes s'aucune a le cuer si tendre
25	*R:* Si le tient . . .
26	*B:* Orendroit sera en agait; *R inserts:* Si le tesmoingne en son corage / Le rousignol per vaselage / Cuer de fame a tant d'outrage
27	*P:* Or a trestot par eritage
29	*P:* Or se hei . . .
30	*B:* Or se plaint . . . ; *P:* Or se rit . . . ; *R:* Or se joue . . .
32	*R:* Or est joieuse . . .
35–36	*R: missing lines; R inserts:* Or aime or est anemie /Or het et or n'aimme mie
41–42	*P: missing lines*
43–44	*R: missing lines*
47–48	*P: missing lines*
51	*BR:* . . . or est peinee
53–54	*R: missing lines; R inserts:* Ainsi se mue son courage / Or requiert l'ombre et puis l'erbage
55–56	*R: missing lines*
57–58	*P: missing lines*
59–60	*R: missing lines*
69	*R:* Or fait besoingne . . .
76	*P:* Ira a dences . . .

78	*B:* . . . or fait le sauvage
81–82	*P: missing lines*
92	*BDP:* En li chastier . . . ; *R:* Ja chastier . . .
93–94	*R: missing lines*
96	*R:* Or se rassiet et puis ressaut
106	*R: missing line*
109	*B: missing line*
112	*B:* Or sera tost et en coulouriee; *P:* Par tens sera bien coloree; *R:* Or est bien tost enluminee
113–14	*P:* missing lines
114	*R:* Or s'en refuit de l'autre part
115–16	*B: missing lines*
115	*R:* Or se rafuble . . .
117–18	*P:* . . . or a baviere / Or est orguelle or est fiere; *R: missing lines*
123–24	*B: missing lines*
124	*R inserts:* Pour estre fresche et colouree / Et quant ele est si atournee
127	*P:* Or vait avant or ce prent garde
131–32	*R: missing lines*
136	*B:* Et se vous die que . . .
137	*B: missing line; R:* tost son chief
138	*R:* Et si ne le tient pas a grief
139	*B:* . . . ou de ceuvrechief; *R: missing line*
140–50	*D: missing lines; lines supplied by P*
140	*R:* Et moult la grieve et ennuie
142	*R inserts:* Tous jours vient estre plus proisi[ee]
145	*B:* Or similie or sa plaire; *R:* Or se polist or sa planoie
146	*B:* . . . or se croie; *R:* or coloie
147	*R:* . . . et puis gete
148	*R:* . . . de bel vel
152	*B:* . . . qui bien sevent faire; *R:* Mais tant i a ne veulent faire
156	*P: missing line*

157   *R:* Or se refait souvent proier
159–76   *B: missing lines*
160   *P:* Chace Halison . . . ; *R:* Fui toi Huet vien ça Marion
162   *R:* Or veut repos . . .
166   *PR:* . . . se poinent
168   *P:* . . . se g'estoie seus; *R:* . . . se fusse escoutes
169   *P:* Et je ansemble vus trovasse; *R:* Et se je dire le vouloie
173–76   *R: missing lines*
176   *P:* Il gaste avoir et cors et ame

Notes

La Contenance des Fames

Lines

1–2	cf. Gen. 1:26.
5–6	cf. Gen. 3:22.
7	lit. "He has lost knowledge," connoting an inability to judge between good and evil.
13–16	lit. "He places his thought and his cares / In woman who cares little / How anything happens / So long as it is according to her wishes."
19	lit. "And let no one think it a fable."
20	cf. French proverbs, "Comme la lune est variable, pensée de femme est variable" (Pineaux 1979: 86; Maloux 1980: 195) and "Souvent femme varie, Bien fol est qui s'y fie" (Pineaux 1979: 86).
23–24	cf. French proverb, "Femme qui donne elle s'abandonne" (Morawski 1925: #736).
27–28	lit. "Woman has inherited a heart that cannot be in one mood."
38	lit. "Now she rejoices, now grows grave."
39	*estable:* firm, strong, stable; lit. "Now she pretends to be firm."
44	lit. "Now she holds herself like a moulting bird."
46	"Now stepmother, now mother." *Marrastre* has the connotation of the wicked stepmother found in folktales.
49	lit. "Now she behaves most properly."
52	lit. "Now wants peace, then wants a fight."
54	*le hale:* sunlight.
56	*four:* public oven; lit. "She runs to the mill, then to the oven," perhaps to indicate the improbability of doing two things at once; cf. the French proverb "One cannot be

both at the oven and at the mill" (Glinsky 1971:81).
Equally so, the author may be referring to another French
proverb, "Au four et au moulin oyt len les nouvelles"
(Morawski 1925: #179), to imply woman's propensity for
gossip.

58   lit. "Runs to the door, then into the room"; lines 57–58
        give the impression of action hither and yon.

60   *conseille:* connotes "whispers" because advice is often
        given in hushed tones.

64   *chamberiere:* chambermaid, housemaid.

67   *voisine:* neighbor.

69   lit. "Now [she] does nothing, now does not cease
        [moving]."

70   *tensera* < *tencier:* to quarrel.

73–74   *tel clerc:* "such and such a fellow" (referring to any
        educated man, not necessarily a cleric); the lines suggest
        that "tel clerc" is the boyfriend of the confidante.

76   *vespres:* vespers; one of the seven daily offices of religious
        devotion that comprise the Divine Office, vespers was the
        sixth canonical hour, recited in the evening.

77   *pelerinage:* pilgrimmage; in the late Middle Ages, the
        pilgrimage to a religious sanctuary became as much a social
        as a religious occasion; cf. Chaucer's *Canterbury Tales.*

79   lit. "The more one studies her, the more one goes mad."

81   *est cornue:* "is horned"; the reference here is to the horn-
        shaped headdresses that were popular in women's dress in
        the late thirteenth century and became even more extreme
        in shape in the fourteenth and fifteenth centuries; see figs. 8
        and 9.

88   lit. "It does not suit her to seek restraints"; *essoingne*
        connotes a legal delay or impediment.

90–91   lit. "What woman thinks, she will do, / Either good or bad
        if ever she can."

93	lit. "That one torments himself, no matter what they say."
96	lit. "Now her heart's at peace, now in turmoil."
101	*escrin:* jewel case; *huche:* chest.
102	lit. "Now she sucks a pear or apple."
107	*queurt* < *courir:* to run
109	cf. French proverb, "Femme rit quand elle peut et pleure quand elle veut" (Maloux 1980: 197).
110	lit. "Her heart changes a lot in a little time."
113	*fart:* eye makeup; *painte:* rouge.
115–16	These lines may refer to the popular style of wearing the hair braided or plaited on either side of the head (see fig. 11).
117	*musel:* probably "veil" or "face-mask"; in a variant of a *fabliau* by Gautier le Leu, *La Veuve,* the widow curses her musel, which suggests it is a widow's veil (Montaiglon and Raynaud n.d. II:343); see also Godefroy 1938: s.v. *musel* V 455 and Livingston 1951: 300–01. *Nasiere:* cf. *nasier:* nostril; probably denotes a mask, such as medieval ladies of high rank wore to protect their faces from sun and dust when traveling or riding (also cf. *naseul:* nose-piece on a medieval helm).
129	*mantel:* coat, usually a costly and sumptuous garment.
131	*sourcot:* surcoat, an outer garment, commonly of rich material, worn during the Middle Ages by high-ranking people of both sexes; see figs. 5–7. Cf. the Middle French proverb, "Les robes de femmes sont si longues et si bien tissues de dissimulation que l'on ne peut reconnaître ce qui est dessous" (Maloux 1980: 192).
133	*cote:* a close-fitting dress or tunic with an ample skirt and large sleeves (see figs. 3, 5); *pelice:* a surcoat lined with fur.
134	lit. "She would think herself very foolish and simple."
137–38	lit. "Undoes and redoes [her outfit] immediately / Now she will turn her headdress."

139   *guimple:* wimple, a piece of cloth worn around the head
       and neck; *chapellot:* a wreath, garland or little hat, see figs.
       2, 5, 10.

145   *se coloie:* moves the head, eyes, like a bird; cf. Middle
       French proverb, "Dame qui moult se mire, peu file"
       (Maloux 201).

147   *redrece < redresser:* to straighten.

148–51 lit. "Now she will again be welcoming / Now she will be
       very attentive / No one could tell you all / Their ways and
       their doings."

155   *cornete:* horn-shaped headdress; see note to line 81.

160   *huche < huchier:* to call loudly, to make come; cf. English
       "Here!" The word has disappeared from modern standard
       French but survives in the Acadian dialect of Nova Scotia.

163–64 lit. "Now goes forward, now goes backward / In such
       guise and in such manner."

170–71 lit. "I would tell it clearly, / All truths are not good to say."

175–76 cf. French proverb "Qui croit et aimme fole femme / Il
       gaste avoir et cors et ame" (Morawski 1925: #1877). This
       proverb was suggested at the beginning of the poem by the
       use of the same vocabulary (l. 12).

Le Bien
des Fames

Le Bien
des Fames

Qui que des fames vous mesdie
Je n'ai talent que mal en die,
C'onques a cortois ne a sage
N'oï de fame dire outrage;
Mes li hom qui est mesdisanz   5
Et envieus et despisanz,
Qui ne crient ne honte ne blasme,
Mesdit des fames et les blasme.
Mes qui los ne pris veut avoir
N'en mesdira por nul avoir;   10
Quar il n'est en cest mont nus hom,
Por que il ait sens ne reson,
Ne doie honor porter a fame
Por l'onor a la haute dame
Que Jhesu Crist tant d'onor fist   15
Que desus les angles l'assist.
Ice est la reson premiere
Par qoi l'en doit fame avoir chiere.
La seconde reson aprés,
Que l'en set bien et loing et prés,   20
Por c'on lor doit porter honor,
Ce est que tuit, grant et menor

The Virtues
of Women

The man who slanders women*
Is a man I must condemn,
For a chap whom one respects
Would never malign the opposite sex;*
But the man who is slanderous,   5
Envious and contemptuous,
Who bears no sense of shame,
Slanders women and deals out blame.
But he who seeks glory and praise
Won't attack a woman's ways;   10
For no member of mankind
With a reasonable mind
Would fail to honor women,
As he honors the blessed Virgin,
Whom Jesus Christ so praised,   15
Whom above the angels he raised.*
This first reason makes it clear
Why men must hold women dear.
A second reason why,
As is known both far and wide,   20
One should honor women all
Is that men, both great and small,

Et un et autre, haut et bas,
Sunt né de fame, n'est pas gas.
Por ce n'en devroit nus mesdire,   *25*
Se il n'est des mauvés li pire,
Et des pïeurs li plus vilains,
S'il estoit quens ou chastelains,
Por qu'il deïst honte de fame,
Si diroie je bien par m'ame,   *30*
Que il feroit vilains de cuer,
Et por ce di je qu'a nul fuer
N'en doit nus dire se bien non;
Tuit cil qui sont de grant renon,
S'il lor portent honor et foi,   *35*
Assez i a reson por qoi
L'en doit fame chiere tenir,
Quar nous veons poi avenir
Cortoisie se n'est par fames.
Bien sai que por l'amor des dames   *40*
Devienent li vilain cortois;
Nus hom s'il lor disoit anois
Ne puet mie bien cortois estre.
Je ne sai clerc, ne lai, ne prestre
Que de fame puist consirrer,   *45*
Se il ne veut trop meserrer
Envers Dieu en mainte maniere.
Par fame destornez en iere.
Fame si fet simples et dous
Cels qui moult sont fel et estous,   *50*
Cels qui sont fel et desdaingneus;
Fame si fet les envïeus
Venir a sens et a mesure;
Fame si est de tel nature

Of humble rank or high,
Were born of woman—that's no lie!
For that reason a man can't curse,   25
If of the bad he's not the worst,
Or the lowest sort of churl,
Even a count or an earl,*
If on women he heaps invective,
I would offer fierce corrective;*   30
He is just a common lout,
Hence I say, on no account,
Should he vilify their name;
Men of great renown and fame
If honorable and guileless*   35
Know sufficient reasons why
We must cherish the female sex;
For it's woman who interjects
The rules of *courtoisie.**
And the love of a fine lady   40
Makes the commoner a lord;*
For no vilifying bawd*
Can become a gentleman.*
Neither cleric, priest, nor layman*
Can from women turn away,   45
If he does not wish to stray
Sinfully from the good Lord;*
Woman educates the wayward,
Woman sweetens and makes mild*
One who's vicious, one who's wild,   50
The scornful and the felonious;
Woman even moves the envious
To find sense and moderation;
She's so well-cast a creation*

Qu'ele fet les coars hardis   55
Et esveillier les endormis;
Moult est fame de grant pooir
Quar par fame, je sai de voir,
Devienent large li aver.
Toz li mondes doit fame amer,   60
Quar de fame vient si granz preus
Que ele fet les mauvés preus.
Fame fet fere les blïaus,
Si fet fere les hommes biaus
Et acesmés et gens et cointes.   65
Toz cels qui d'eles sont acointes,
Si fet fere chevaleries
Et les beles joustes furnies;
Fame si fet lances brisier,
Et les granz tornois commencier.   70
Fame fet fere noveaus sons
E dire sonez e chansons;
Si fet fere chapiaus de flors
A cels qui aiment par amors;
Si fait karoler et dancier   75
E fait estroitement chantier;
Fame si fet a mienuit
Les bachelers plains de deduit
Aler aus festes et aus veilles.
Fame si fet tant de merveilles   80
Que la moitié n'en conteroie,
Se grant entente n'i metoie.
Moult doit fame estre chiere tenue,
Par li est toute gent vestue;
Bien sai que fame file et oevre   85
Les dras dont l'en se vest et cuevre;

That she makes the coward brave   55
And awakes the slumbering knave;*
Such astounding powers has she
That she can (I tell you truly)
Make the miser give up greed.
Let us cherish her indeed,*   60
For she prompts great acts of prowess,
Conjures great deeds out of cowardice.*
To her we owe the robes* we wear
That flatter men so we appear
Attractive and refined.   65
Those acquainted with womankind
Shall be knights of chivalry,*
In the jousts* keep company;
In her honor lances break,
Tourneys* flourish for her sake.   70
For her, lovely songs are made,
Ballads, motets, serenades;
Floral wreaths are plaited merrily
For those who love her tenderly;
For her the lively round is danced*   75
And intricate melodies advanced;*
For her sake at the midnight hour,
Exuberant bachelors in their flower
Celebrate, and feast, and revel.
Women work so many marvels   80
That I could only tell you half,
Unless I labored at the task.
With women we are blessed,*
By their work, we are dressed;
They spin, weave, and prepare   85
The clothes that people wear;*

Et si oevre tot a devise
Les garnements de saint eglise,
Et toissus d'or et dras de soie.
Et por ce di je, ou que je soie,   90
A toz cels qui orront cest conte:
Que de fame ne dïent honte,
Quar si comme li sages dist,
N'est pas sages qui en mesdist;
Que aus fames honor ne porte   95
La seue honor doit estre morte.

Explicit le Bien des fames

And they work hard to provide
Splendid raiments for Christ's bride,*
Also gold cloth, silk brocade.
Thus the plea that I have made   90
To all to whom I speak my mind:*
Do not womankind malign,
For as wise men have made clear
Only fools at women sneer.
Who leaves their honor unsung, unsaid,   95
His own honor must be dead.*

End of the Virtues of Women

Variants

Le Bien des Fames

L = London; *P* = Paris; *R* = Rouen

Lines

7	*L:* Mes i a nus hon qui guere vaillent 8; *R:* Mes i a nus hom qui criemme blame
14	*L:* Pour l'amor . . .
29	*R:* Pour ce qu'il mesdie de fame
30	*L: missing line*
32	*L:* Car je fai bien que a nul fuer
36	*R:* Or oez la reson pourquoi
38	*R:* Nus hon ne pourroit maintenir
40	*R:* Bien savez sans l'enneur a dames
42	*R:* I le covient amer enchois; *L:* Nus hom si n'a amme ancois
44	*R:* Quer on ne vi ne clerc ne prestre
46	*R:* Si ne veut malement meserrer
48	*L:* Par famme devient denneire; *R:* Quar fame fet mut simple chiere
49–54	*R: missing lines*
57–64	*R: missing lines*
65–68	*P: missing lines*
69–70	*LR: missing lines*
71–72	*P: missing lines*
75–76	*P: missing lines*
78	*L:* Les esveliez . . .
85	*L:* Car famme file et si oeuvre
87–88	*P: missing lines*
90–96	*R: missing lines*

Notes

Le Bien des Fames

Lines

1 *mesdie,* infinitive *mesdire;* see lines 5, 8, 10, 95. The word and its cognates are very strong in their connotation of "gossip, lies, calumnies." Such speech was, of course, frowned upon in courtly society. Andreas Capellanus condemns gossip (1941: 93–94) and excludes such behavior from courtly society in his precepts of love: "Be mindful completely to avoid falsehood" and "Thou shalt speak no evil" (82–83).

3–4 lit. "For not once by a courtly or wise man / Have I heard womankind maligned."

16 The phrase may be taken to refer to the Coronation of the Virgin, commonly depicted in manuscripts and on the tympana of church portals from the twelfth century on. In scenes of Mary as the Queen of Heaven, she is seen standing on a crescent moon, wearing a crown bearing twelve stars, as described in the apocalyptic vision of Rev. 12:1. The Coronation of Mary shows the Mother of God seated on a throne next to her son, who places the crown of glory on her head. The historical meaning of the Virgin's Triumph derives from biblical passages: 1 Kings 2:19, the Song of Songs, and Ps. 44, and this subject was treated widely in the medieval exegetical literature, where Mary was referred to as "Queen of the world," "elevated" to share Christ's throne in heaven. See Katzenellenbogen 1959: 50–58; Verdier 1980 passim; and Mâle 1958: IV, part 1.

27–28 lit. "And the lowest of the worst / If he be count or *castellan* (lord of a manor)." Note the social contrast between commoners (*vilains*) and the nobility (*quens*). See also lines 31 and 41.

30   lit. "And upon my soul, I would truly say."

35   lit. "As they show them [i.e., women] honor and trust."

37–39   lit. "One must hold woman dear / For we see little of courtesy brought forth / If not for women."

39   *cortoisie:* courtliness, pertaining to the code of behavior that governed the manners of aristocratic men and women during the Middle Ages; chivalric derives from *chevalier*, indicating that the medieval gentleman was first and foremost a warrior on a horse (*cheval*). For a twelfth-century view of the role of women within the bounds of the chivalric code, see Andreas Capellanus 1941.

41   *devienent li vilain cortois:* see Andreas Capellanus 1941: 31: "Now it is the effect of love that . . . it can endow a man even of the humblest birth with nobility of character."

42   Though in modern usage "bawd" usually refers to a female prostitute, it originally designated a male panderer (*Oxford English Dictionary*, s.v. *Bawd*).

43   lit. "Cannot ever be truly courtly."

44   lit. "I know no cleric, layman, or priest": the distinction here is between members of the clerical class and the laity, and then between the clergy proper and those men who had taken lower orders, either to study in the schools or, in fact, to become priests. There is a considerable literature in the Middle Ages on the advantages and disadvantages of a priest or layman as a lover (see Oulmont 1972).

46–47   lit. "If he does not wish to stray too far / From God in any way."

49   The repeated use of the causative *faire* (see also ll. 53, 55, 62, 63, 64, 67, 69, 71, 73, 75, 76, 77, 80) emphasizes the role of woman as a civilizing agent: she *makes* men affable, she *makes* the envious reasonable, she has fine clothes *made*, and so on.

54   lit. "Woman is of such a nature."

55–56   cf. the episode in Chrétien de Troyes's romance *Lancelot* (1970), where the hero's strength and courage in battle are ignited by a brief glimpse of his adored mistress, Guinevere.

60   lit. "All the world must love woman."

62   lit. "She makes the bad, worthy (noble)."

63   *bliaus:* long tunic, worn over armor.

67   lit. "She launches military expeditions." See note to line 39; the English word *knight* derives from the Anglo-Saxon *cniht,* the equivalent of the French *chevalier.*

68   *joustes:* individual combat between mounted combatants armed with blunted lances or swords.

70   The tourneys or tournaments were popular medieval entertainments involving jousts and other war games. For a prize bestowed by the lady of the tourney, each contestant in the joust tried to unseat his opponent or break his opponent's lance.

75   *karoler:* to dance in a circle; to have fun.

76   lit. "Makes people sing narrowly." The medieval period prized complexity in musical composition. An example of such complexity would be that a voice was said to enter in a *stretto,* or "narrow"—in other words, one entered before the preceding voice had finished stating the theme; see Sachs 1955: 97.

83   lit. "Much must woman be held dear."

85–86   lit. "Well I know that woman spins and works / The cloth with which one is clothed and covered." There is an interesting passage in the twelfth-century romance by Chrétien de Troyes *Le Chevalier au lion* (1971), in which the hero rescues a group of maidens forced to spin and weave. Women dominated the cloth-making profession until the end of the eighteenth century, performing most of the preliminary processes (such as combing and carding of

wool) and all of the spinning (the English word *spinster*
derives from this exclusively female occupation; see Fiero
essay).

88   lit. "The ornaments of the holy church." *Garnements:*
ornaments, vestments. In medieval typology, the Church
and Mary were both referred to as "the Bride of Christ."
The first parallel was based on passages in the New
Testament, especially Eph. 5:25 and Rev. 21:2; the second
derived from the Songs of Songs and Ps. 44 (see note to l.
16). The bride in the Song of Songs was identified with
both the Church and the Virgin Mary. Innumerable
passages in medieval exegesis refer to the likeness between
Mary and the Church in their close, permanent, and loving
union with the Savior. See Bugge 1975: 59–79.

90–91   lit. "And that is why I say wherever I may be / To all those
who will hear this tale."

95–96   These lines seem to have been a commonplace in the sparse,
pro-feminine literature of medieval France; see Meyer
1877: 501.

Le Blasme
des Fames

Le Blasme
des Fames

(Les Propretés des
Femmes en Romaunz)

Oez seignurs e escutez
E a ma parole entendez:
Ki en femme trop met sa cure,
Sovent serra saunz honure;
Ki femme aime ou femme prise   5
Sovent en vient a gref juïse;
Ki femme ou femine creit
Sa mort brace e sa mort beit;
Senz pris e sanz lüer se vent,
Il fet la hard dunt il se pent.   10
Qui ces vers avera en remembrance
Doutera femme plus que nul lance.
Ki mesprist primes, hom u femme?
Ki nous getta de notre regne?
Ki tendi a autre la poume: 15
Home a femme ou femme a home?
Pur quai va femme a chief covert
E li home li son apert?
Pur quai? pur la hunte de pecché,
Q'ele nous getta de notre fé.   20
Pur ceo qe femme out fieble sens
L'enginnat primes li serpens;

The Vices
of Women

*(The Characteristics of
Women in French)*

Listen to me, lords, I pray,
Lend an ear to what I say:*
Who too much trusts in womankind,
Often leaves honor far behind;
Who loves or prizes womankind   5
Often ends up much maligned;*
He who trusts them one or all
Drinks the hemlock, tastes the gall;*
He's self-demeaning and a dope,
He hangs himself by his own rope.   10
He who keeps these lines in mind
Fears swords less than womankind.*
Ask: who first sinned—man or woman?
Who got us exiled from the Garden?
Who offered the apple to whom:*   15
Woman to man or man to woman?
Why does woman cover her head
While man leaves his bare instead?
Why? Because of the sinner's shame:
She drove us from our first domain.*   20
Because of woman's weaker wit
She fell into the snake's gambit;*

Cil qui ne pout foul espleiter
Ad perempli per le mulier;
Puis lui donna une dowarie   25
Ke fust unfant en toute sa vie;
Otriat lui en gereisoun
Que tut tens fust encontre reison;
Donat lui orgoille e envie,
Le foundement de felunie;   30
Ensi la fist a son semblant,
Sa fai lui tendi meintenant.
Puis qe li monde fust furmé,
Comença femme cruealté;
E cum plus durra iceste vie   35
Crestrunt ses enginz e sa folie.
Femme ad descorde en sun corage
Pur corrumpir son mariage;
Femme est achesun de tuz maus,
Femme engendre les ires morteus.   40
Femme fet descuerer les amis,
De deuz freres fet enemis;
Femme depart les fiz del pere,
A lui se treit, tout lui sa mere.
Femme fet bien par coverture,   45
Maudehé ait sa demaine nature;
Femme par sa douce parole,
Atret li home e puis l'afole;
Femme est dehors religiouse,
Dedanz poignaunt e venimose;   50
Femme afole le plus savaunt,
Del plus riche fet pain queraunt;
Femme engendre bataille e guere,
Exile gent de gaste tere;

Her better half the lesser fool,
The snake used woman as his tool;*
The dowry bestowed upon the wife   25
Was childishness throughout her life;
He granted her as remedy
A loathing for rationality;
He gave her pride and envy,
The building-blocks for felony;   30
The serpent made her in his image,
And she to him now renders homage.
Since the world's nativity,
Woman has sowed depravity;*
However long we all survive   35
Her tricks and folly will thrive.
The discord in a woman's heart
Corrupts marriage from the start;
Of every evil she's the root,
The tree bears anger as its fruit.*   40
She sets friends against one another,
Turning brother against brother;
She cleaves the father from the son,
She robs the mother's nest of one.*
Outwardly she's well-behaved,   45
But by her nature, she's depraved;
Her words are sweetness sugar-clad
To lure a man and drive him mad;
On the outside she's religious,
On the inside keen and venomous;   50
She makes the wisest lose his head,
She makes the richest beg his bread;
Woman fosters strife and wars,
And exiles men from ruined shores;

Femme ard chasteus e prent citez,   55
Enfudre tours e fermetez.
Femme fet fere les turneez,
Femme fet trere les espees,
Femme commence les estreez,
E meintent les melleez;   60
Femme engine en poi d'ure
Dount un[e] tere tout ploure.
Femme medle venim od mel,
En douce let fet beivre fel.
Femme enlace joefnes e vieles,   65
A simples homes tout ses bienz.
Femme par sa douce parole
Atret li home e puis l'afole.
Femme est aigne pur primes tundre,
Femme est serpent par grefment poindre,   70
Femme est lyuns pur seignurer,
Femme est leopard pur devurer,
Femme est goupille pur deceivre,
Femme est urs pur coups receivre,
Femme est chien pur aveir grant sens,   75
Femme est chate pur mordre as denz,
Femme est rate pur confundre,
Femme est suriz pur sei repondre;
Femme est dedens heriçuns,
Defors simple cum colums;   80
Femme est faucoun pur surmonter
E esperver pur daunteler;
Femme est mesenge pur tencer,
Muissun pur sovent kauker;
Femme est le jour merle e mauvis,   85
E a vespre cauvesurriz;

Castles she burns, cities defeats,   55
Destroys the towers and the keeps.
Woman's the reason tourneys are born,*
Woman's the reason swords are worn,
Enmity she instigates,
And combat she perpetuates;   60
The schemes she quickly engineers
Can drown a countryside in tears.*
With honey woman mixes bile,
The sweetest milk she will defile.
Both young and old she'll captivate.   65
She picks clean the most innocent bait.*
Her words are sweetness sugar-clad
To lure a man and drive him mad.
First, simple as a lamb is she,*
But venomous as a snake* can be,   70
Imperious as a lion* is she,
Voracious as a leopard* she,
Deceitful as a fox* is she,
Combative as a bear* is she,
The canine's* sharper sense has she,   75
As sharp-toothed as a cat* is she,
Destructive as a rat* is she,
As sneaky as a mouse* is she;
On the inside like a hedgehog's hide
But gentle as a dove* outside;   80
As masterful as a falcon* she,
A sparrowhawk demure as can be;*
As quarrelsome as a titmouse* she,
As lecherous as a sparrow* she,
A blackbird or a thrush by day,   85
A bat when dark is on its way;*

Femme est huan esstacé,
Le jour se muce, la nuyt est wacé.
Femme est funteine desur la veie
Ke tuz receit e tuz avoie;   90
Femme est marchié de tele nature,
Tut tens bate e tut tens dure;
Femme est taverne qe faute,
Ki ke vienge e qi qe vaute;
Femme est enfer qe tut receit,   95
Tut tens ad seif e tut tens beit.
Femme ne set estre fel,
Femme doune mauveise consel;
Femme n'a garde sa parole
K'ele ne dit sovent qe fole;   100
Femme ad un art plus qe deable
K'ele ne set estre estable;
Femme est baude de curage eschange,
Hui privé, demain estrange.
Femme fet hunt' a meint franc hom   105
Pur meins qe ne vaut un[e] poume;
Femme set ben li fol atrere
Quaunt ele quide sun prou fere;
Femme lui fet mult bele chere
E puis lui fet la luse derere;   110
Femme li tout s'il ad rien,
Ne dirrat de lui jamés bien,
E nul ne se puet de lui esgarder
Quaunt ele li vout enginner;
Femme, si ele veut mester,   115
Nul ne se pot de ceo retrere;
Femme si hardement surmunte

She is the owl that terrifies,*
By day she hides, at night she flies.
She's like a roadside watering hole,
Attracting each and every soul;*   90
She's a bargain, without peer,
Always slugging she'll persevere;*
She's a tavern-keeper* who
Rips off each who passes through;
She's a hell-mouth that is cursed   95
With an all-consuming thirst.*
Woman shuns fidelity,*
Gives evil counsel readily;
Woman's deaf to what she's saying,*
All her chatter's foolish braying;   100
She's more artful than the devil
And she's equally unfaithful;*
Woman's a creature with a fickle heart,*
She's close to you now, tomorrow she'll part.
She'll shame the finest man on earth,   105
For a bauble not an apple's worth;
How readily she snares the fool,
If she can profit, he's her tool;
She gives him her good-time routine,
Then turns around and shaves him clean;*   110
She'll strip him right down to his skin,
And say not one good word of him;
A man cannot withstand her guile
Once she has picked him for her wile;
Her will to power will prevail,   115
She vanquishes most any male;*
She overcomes in easy course

Ice pour travail e hunte;
Femme ayme deuz jours ou treis,
A la quarte quert un tut freis.   *120*
Fous est qui en femme s'afie,
Ore eyme, sempres ublie;
Ceo dist l'em de femmes foles:
"Gardum nous de lur escoles."
Ore vous ai dit de lur vies,   *125*
Fuoums de lur cumpaignies.
Pur Dieu, seignurs, uncore vous requer,
Gardum nos cors de mal encumbrer;
Ne creez femme car ceo est lur mester,
Mentir, trahir, e gent enpoisoner;   *130*
E tuz maus qe home pot dire
Ne pöent suffir' a femme en ire.
Ire de femme fet a douter,
Mut se deit chescun garder;
Car la ou plus amé averat,   *135*
Ileoc plus tost se vengerat.
Cum de legier vient lur amur,
De plus leger revient lur haur;
E plus dure lur enemisté
Qe ne fet lur amisté;   *140*
L'amur sevent amesurer,
Haur ne sevent atemprer.
Aitant cum eles sunt en ire,
Jeo ne ose de eus si bien non dire.

Unde versus:
Qi capit uxorem capit absque quiete laborem.   *145*
longum languorem. lacrimas cum lite dolorem.

All shame, all qualms, and all remorse;
She loves for two days or for three,
On day four, seeks new company.   *120*
Crazy is he who trusts a woman,*
She loves him now and then forgets him;
Of wayward women the wise man says:
"O Lord protect us from their ways."
Now that I've told you of womankind,   *125*
Let's flee and leave them far behind!
In Lord God's name I beg you still,
Let's keep our bodies safe from ill;
Don't follow her whose main devices
Are lies, betrayal, and toxic vices.*   *130*
And all the words a man can say
Won't make her anger go away;
Woman's anger makes one fearful,
To avoid it, let's be careful;
For wherever she has given her all   *135*
There she'll vent her vengeful gall.
As quickly as her love will burn,
More quickly will her ire return;
More lasting is her enmity
Than ever lasts her amity;   *140*
Love she knows well how to dole,
Hatred she cannot control.
Woman lives in constant anger,
Do I even dare harangue her?*

Whence the verse:*
He who takes a wife trades peace for strife.   *145*
Long weariness, despair, oppress his life,

pondus valde grave. verbosum vas sine clave.
quod nulli claudit. sed detegit omne quod audit.
uxorem duxi quod semper postea luxi.

A heavy load, a barrel full of chatter,
Uncorkable, her gossip makes a clatter,
Now, ever since I took a wife,
Calamity has marred my life.

Variants

Le Blasme des Fames

C = Cambridge; F = Florence; L = London; O = Oxford; P = Paris 1593; Q = Paris 837; R = Rouen; W = Westminster

Title L: Incipit tractatus de bonitate et malitia mulierum; *PQ:* Le Blasme des fames; *W:* De la condition des femmes

Lines

4	*L:* Oiez sa mort et sa dreiture; *F:* Oiez sa mort et sa nature
5	*L:* Qy coveyte ou femme preyse
9	*F:* . . . et sans loect savent
14	*F:* Qui nescoilli in cest saint regne
15	*F:* Liquelz tolli primier la pome
19	*F:* Por le pechie ce m'est avis
20	*F:* Qui nos gitta del paradis
23	*F:* Ce que por hom ne poet plorer
24	*F:* Si os plorai por la mollier
25	*F:* Poi li dona in duelise
26	*F:* Que fost noscians an tote guise
31	*C:* Issi la fist a sei clinaunt; *F* 37
32	*F:* Cel fei en ont tuit li enfant
39	*PW: missing line; L:* Femme est racyne . . .
40	*PW: missing line; QR:* Par fame sort guerres et maus
41	*PW: missing line*
42	*PW: missing line; QR:* Et les fet mortels anemis
43	*PW: missing line*
44	*PW: missing line*
49	*C:* femme est dedens; *corrected from F*
50	*C:* dehors . . . ; *corrected from F*
54	*F:* Com sis enging devasta terre; *L:* Occyre gentz destrure terre

56	*F:* Feme fait fondre fermetes; *L:* Femme refuse fermetes
58	*LPQRW:* Et trere coutiaus et espees
61–62	*L:* femme engendre en poi de houre / dount tute la countré emploure 35–36
65–66	*sic; the couplet does not rhyme, but no other manuscript has a similar couplet*
67	*L:* Femme par sa fauce parole
68	*L:* Blaundist le honme . . .
70	*LPW: missing line*
73	*PW: missing line*
74	*PW: missing line; F:* Femme est orse por globens bevre
75	*C:* . . . chien pur sens; *F:* Feme est ghies . . .
77	*LPW: missing line*
78	*C:* respondre; *Q:* 42; *R:* 40
79	*F:* Et est dedens yncorns
82	*L:* . . . pur haut voler
83	*C:* pur tenir; *F:* 120
86	*FLPW: missing line; QR:* Fame est la nuit . . .
87	*LPW: missing line; F:* Feme est avaire feme est stassaie; *QR:* . . . feme est fressaie
88	*LPW: missing line; F:* Le jor se drot la not s'esveie; *QR:* Par jour se mue la nuit s'esgaie
89	*PW: missing line; Q:* Fame est taverne . . .
90	*C:* Ke tuz receit et tuz afaie; *F:* Que tot rechut fuit a sa joie; *QR:* 52; *PW: missing line*
91	*C:* macé; *LPW: missing line; O:* Fame est de mal arret et de male nature; *QR:* 47
92	*LWP: missing line*
93	*PW: missing line*
94	*PW: missing line; F:* . . . qui chevaut
95	*PW: missing line*
96	*C:* nous; *F:* 130; *PW: missing line*
103	*F:* . . . de qui n'et çage
112	*F:* Tot tems prent ne dira neon
115	*F:* Feme si velt tot sachier

Notes

Le Blasme des Fames

Title	This piece is generally known as the "Blasme des femmes" (the title provided in the two Paris manuscripts [837 and 1593]). The second title given here is that of the Cambridge manuscript, which provided the text for this edition.

Lines

1–2	The opening lines call attention to the orality of the *dit* as a genre. Note the imperative *Oez* ("hear"), *escutez* ("listen"), and *entendez* ("harken").
6	lit. "Often comes to a sad judgment [on her account]."
8	lit. "Embraces death, drinks his demise."
12	lit. "Will fear woman more than any lance."
15	cf. Gen. 3:6.
17–20	lit. "Why does woman have her head covered / And man his bare? / Why? For the shame of the sin, / That drove us from our faith." Saint Paul refers to the practice of women covering their heads while at prayer as a sign of subordination: "Every man praying or prophesying with his head covered, disgraces his head. But every woman praying or prophesying with her head uncovered, disgraces her head, for it is the same as if she were shaven. But if it is a disgrace for a woman to have her hair cut off or her head shaved, let her cover her head. A man indeed ought not to cover his head, because he is the image and the glory of God. But woman is the glory of man" (1 Cor. 11:4–7).
22	*enginnat < enginer:* to invent, manufacture, deceive, seduce; see lines 53, 61, 114, and also line 36, *enginz:* skill, trick.
21–24	The serpent or snake, "more crafty than any wild creature that God had made," was a popular medieval symbol of

134

evil, biblically synonymous with Satan (Gen. 3:1–16).
Medieval theologians held that Satan chose Eve as the
instigator of disobedience because she was more credulous
than Adam and inferior to him in reasoning; see Fiero
essay. Lines 23–24: lit. "Man he could not seduce alone /
[The serpent] accomplished it by means of the woman."

34   lit. "Woman began her cruelty."

40   lit. "Woman engenders mortal anger."

44   lit. "Draws man to her and takes him from his mother"; cf.
      Gen. 2:24, renewed in Matt. 19:5, Mark 10:7, and Eph.
      5:31; cf. also Prov. 19:26.

57   Compare the *Bien des femmes*, lines 66–70; see the note to
      line 70.

61–62 lit. "Woman schemes in little time / For which reason
      everyone in the country weeps."

65–66 These two lines do not rhyme in the French text. It is
      possible that an earlier text read at line 65 *vieus* ("old").
      Though *vieux* does not rhyme with *biens*, because *u* and *n*
      are easily confused in medieval manuscripts, a medieval
      proofreader would see an eye-rhyme and not try to correct
      the text.

69–84 The author uses the construction "Femme est . . . pur . . ."
      ("Woman is . . . for . . . ") as in "Femme est leopard pur
      devurer" ("Woman is a leopard for devouring"), thus
      creating a series of metaphors, rendered in our translation
      as similes. Women are compared to beasts in other
      misogynic vernacular poems of the Middle Ages, for
      example, the anonymous verses that appear in the margins
      of a fourteenth-century manuscript, Rome: Vatican Library
      Regina Lat. 1659, f. 98 (Merrilees 1971: 7).

69–70 lit. "Woman is a lamb for fleecing, / Woman is a snake to
      cause grief." These lines contrast the qualities of innocence
      and guile in the characters of the lamb, a traditional symbol
      of innocence (associated with Jesus), and the snake, the
      popular medieval symbol for malignant evil (associated

with Satan; see notes to ll. 21–24). The Latin word for
lamb (*agnus*) was thought to come from the Greek word
meaning "chaste" (Isidoro de Sevilla 1951: xii, 12). In
medieval bestiaries, the lamb was associated with both
Jesus and his flock, and thus with Christian virtue in
general.

71   The sense of this line is that woman is a lion in order to
rule over others. Medieval bestiaries viewed the Latin word
for lion (*leo*) as a corruption of the Greek word for "king."
Though the lion carried positive associations of invincible
power and magnanimity (Guillaume le Clerc 1936: 14–16),
it also represented retributive justice, fierceness, and cruelty
(Rowland 1973: 119–23; McCulloch 1962: 138–40).

72   In the Middle Ages the leopard was considered a fierce and
ruthless beast of prey (Friedmann 1980: 202). The
medieval bestiary calls the leopard "a parti-coloured
species, very swift and strongly inclined to bloodshed"
(White 1954: 13). In homiletic literature the leopard was
associated with the anti-Christ (Rowland 1973: 117).

73   Latin versions of the *Physiologus* refer to the fox as "a
figure of the devil" (*Physiologus* 1979: 27–28), and the
medieval bestiary identified the animal as "fraudulent and
ingenious" (White 1954: 53). Reynard the Fox, the hero of
the popular medieval tale *Roman de Renart*, was well
known for his pranks, including the practice of playing
dead in order to catch unsuspecting prey (McCulloch 1962:
119), figurative of Satan.

74   lit. "Woman is a bear to receive blows." The bear's
reputation for angry aggression was long-standing. Saint
Augustine saw the bear as typifying the devil because of its
strength (Friedmann 1980: 197). The medieval bestiary
relates that bears attack bulls by seizing their horns and
wounding their snouts (McCulloch 1962: 95). A symbol of
evil in Christian commentary, the bear was also considered
lustful and was often identified with fornication and

dissolute behavior (Rowland 1973: 32–33). In parts of medieval France, Candlemas celebrations included the mock attack on a "lustful bear" (Davis 1975: 137); it may be in this sense that line 74 is intended. Besides the literary and homiletic traditions, however, the bear's reputation for toughness and resistance to capture would have been well known to hunters (Gaston Phébus warned that bear hunting required the efforts of at least two well-armed men, 1971: 230).

75   lit. "Woman is a dog as to having great intelligence." The dog received "mixed press" during the Middle Ages. In medieval allegory it was a symbol of fidelity and was praised as a creature of great intelligence. However, the dog also appears in medieval art and literature as an attribute of envy, one of the seven deadly sins, and as one of the five senses, that of smell. The bestiary relates that the dog returns to its own vomit (McCulloch 1962: 110). Medieval conduct books warned nuns to avoid the sinister "hound of hell" (Rowland 1973: 60–61). Medieval devotional tracts picture dogs as scavengers and thieves (Marrow 1977: 176–78). In the second redaction to Gratian's *Decretum*, Bartholomeus Brixiensis (fl. 1250) compares the promiscuity of prostitutes to canine love: "Dogs indeed copulate indifferently and indiscriminately" (quoted in Bullough and Brundage 1982: 150). In the context of lines 69–88, it would seem that the author of the *Blasme* alludes to these negative attributes.

76   The cat is described in the medieval bestiary as "catus" because she catches things (*acaptura*) and because she lies in wait (*captat*) (White 1954: 90–91). Associated with the choleric disposition among the four humors, the cat was symbolic of "choleric savagery" (Friedmann 1980: 162). In the medieval world the cat also symbolized the Devil; heretics were frequently denounced for worshipping Lucifer in the shape of a cat and accused of copulating with

the creature as well (hence the association between cats and witches). The modern expression "cathouse" derives from these sexual associations (Rowland 1973: 50–53).

77   lit. "Woman is a rat to confound [destroy or subvert]." Noted for its destructiveness, the rat was a medieval symbol of decay (Rowland 1973: 136). Even in antiquity rats were considered savage and were thought to have strong teeth that could eat through iron (Aelianus 1958: 345). The rat was also perceived as a type for Satan and his demons, which are often pictured in medieval art with the long narrow tails, sharp teeth, and claws of rats.

78   lit. "Woman is a mouse when it comes to hiding." Like the rat, the mouse was regarded as destructive and undependable (Isidoro de Sevilla 1951: 295; Friedmann 1980: 271–72) and was associated with thieves who, by stealth, greedily store up mundane wealth. Considered as unusually fertile, the mouse was another favorite medieval symbol for lechery, especially female lechery (Rowland 1973: 127–28).

79–80 These lines contrast the threatening, predatory character of woman with her innocent and gentle appearance. The spikes of the hedgehog are inside the woman, where they cannot be seen; on the exterior, woman is like a dove, which the bestiary refers to as "a very sweet bird / Without guile and bitterness" (Guillaume le Clerc 1936: ll. 2900–01). In medieval lore, the dove signified Jesus, the Holy Ghost (White 1954: 160), and a variety of church-related concepts (Rowland 1977: 47), while the hedgehog symbolized Satan (the hedgehog's attack on the farmer's vineyard, related in the bestiary, was likened to the devil's attack on the Christian soul; see Guillaume le Clerc 1936: ll. 1155–58). Hence, the message of these lines is that womankind is superficially innocent but inherently dangerous.

81   The falcon was a popular medieval bird of prey, trained for
hunting. As the emperor Frederick II of Germany noted in
his famous treatise *The Art of Falconry* (ca. 1250), the
falcon eagerly attacks birds larger than itself, such as the
eagle. As aristocratic sport, falconry was especially
associated with upper-class women. John of Salisbury
observed, "The inferior sex excels in the hunting of
birds . . . [since] inferior creatures are always more prone
to rapine" (Pike 1938: 17).

82   lit. "And a sparrowhawk for taming." The sparrowhawk
was noted for its harshness toward its young, which,
according to Isidoro de Sevilla, it pushed out of the nest as
soon as the fledglings were able to fly (1951: 313). Like the
falcon, the sparrowhawk was used for hunting and was
noted for its unerring skill at attacking larger birds
(Frederick II 1955: 127–28).

83   Although the titmouse does not appear in traditional Latin
bestiaries, it is included in Pierre de Beauvais's long version
of the bestiary that dates from ca. 1215 (McCulloch 1962:
203–04), where it is noted for its curiosity. The titmouse
was also known for its talkative nature and its penchant for
gossip (Friedmann 1980: 299).

84   Like the falcon and sparrowhawk, the sparrow does not
appear in Latin and French bestiaries; it was nevertheless a
popular medieval symbol for wantonness and lechery.
Medieval French puns play on the association between the
words for sparrow (*moineau*) and monk (*moine*). In some
European folktales the Devil assumed the shape of a
sparrow (Rowland 1977: 157–58).

85–86   These lines draw still another contrast between the positive
and negative aspects of woman. Both day birds, the
blackbird and the thrush were prized for their sweet and
melodic sounds (McCulloch 1962: 96–97). The former was
considered a particularly agreeable caged pet and was also

associated with love, sensual passion, and death (Rowland
1977: 11–12). The bat, on the other hand, was viewed as a
wholly unpleasant and ignoble bird, whose Latin name
(*vespertilio*) was thought to come from the word for
eventide (*vesper*) (McCulloch 1962: 94). Medieval
preachers linked the bat's alleged blindness to moral
obtuseness and regarded bats as symbols of hypocrisy and
duplicity (Rowland 1977: 7).

87   lit. "Woman is an owl tied up [or nailed up]." The
reference here may be to the folk practice of killing an owl
and nailing it up to ward off evil (*The Owl and the
Nightingale* 1960: ll. 1605 ff.). Throughout the Middle
Ages the owl carried sinister attributes. The *Physiologus*
describes the owl as a dirty bird that prefers darkness to
light (1979: 10–12). Moralizing accounts of the bird
emphasized its preference for darkness as symbolic of those
who reject Jesus (Friedmann 1980: 276; McCulloch 1962:
147). Isidoro de Sevilla thought the owl slothful and noted
that the Latin name for owl (*noctua*) derived from its night
(*nox*) flight (Isidoro de Sevilla 1951: 311). Associated with
graveyards and evil spirits, the owl was a portent of death
and a type of Satan (Rowland 1977: 118–19). Frederick II
observed that owls are rapacious birds that "prey upon the
young of other birds" (Frederick II 1955: 29). Thus, like
many of the creatures to which the author of the *Blasme*
compares woman, the owl was a predator.

89–90   lit. "She's a fountain on the road / That welcomes all,
whatever their load [or: and leads all astray]." *Avoier* has
two possible meanings: (1) to lead, to put on the way (cf.
Jubinal 1835: "to lead astray," 81), and (2) to empty. The
second meaning relates to the image of the fountain, a
common metaphor for the vagina. In the *fabliau* "De la
damoiselle qui ne pooit oïr parler de foutre" ("The Maiden
Who Could Not Bear to Hear Intercourse Mentioned"), the

bashful girl offers her "fontenele" to quench the thirst of her bridegroom's "horse" (Montaiglon and Raynaud n.d.: III, 84). In another version, "De la pucelle qui abevra le polain" ("The Maiden Who Gave the Colt Water"), the virgin describes her vagina as "ma fountaine, / Qui toz jors sort et ja n'est pleine" ("My fountain / Which always flows and is never full"; Montaiglon and Raynaud n.d.: IV, 204). See Cooke 1976: 16, 68, 176–77 and Rigg 1986: 90–91. Lines 89–90 should also be read as an inversion of the positive image of Mary, who was traditionally regarded as "the fountain of living waters," a reference derived from the Song of Songs 4:12 and Psalms 36:19.

91–92   lit. "She's a bargain of such a nature / She always fights and always endures."

93   lit. "Woman is [like a] tavern. . . ." In the Middle Ages women were associated with the production, as well as with the retail sales, of food and drink, hence with tavern-keeping (Lehmann 1952: 457; Power 1975: 67–69; Gies and Gies 1978: 175, 177).

95–96   lit. "Woman is a hell that receives all / She's always thirsty and always drinking." Throughout the Middle Ages, hell was pictured as a gaping mouth that devoured sinners destined for eternal damnation. The image of the hell-mouth probably originated in early medieval Celtic apocalyptic literature, where hell is described as a hollow hill; see Patch 1950: 109.

97   *fel < fidelis:* faithful, loyal, sincere. In central Old French, the word was "feal, feeil," but the Anglo-Norman dialect could reduce the vowels one step further (see Pope 1954: §1131).

99   The French spelling of this line may represent the scribe's attempt to record pronunciation, illustrating in "garde" (for "gart de") the effacement of final consonant *t* (Pope 1954: §1199 and §1232), combined with the practice of

running together words linked in the phrase (Pope 1954: §§1201–02).

102   lit. "She does not know how to be stable." See the *Contenance,* line 39 and note.

103   lit. "Woman is eager to change her heart."

110   lit. "And then acts like a pike behind him." The reference here is to the predatory nature of the pike, which frequently attacks and devours other fish.

115–16   lit. "Woman if she wants the task / No one can refuse her." For similar rhymes in Anglo-Norman, see Pope 1954: §1135.

121   On this proverbial line, see Pfeffer essay and Pineaux 1979: 86.

129–30   lit. "Do not believe women, for this is their task / To lie, to steal, and to poison people."

143–44   lit. "As long as they are angry / I dare not say of them [anything] but good."

145–49   These Latin hexameters are attached to the *Blasme des fames* in the Cambridge manuscript. They circulated widely and are found in other manuscripts of the period (see Walther 1959–69: 15407 and 19943), as well as in early printed collections of Latin proverb literature (Walther 1966: 23903–04).

Appendix

The following lines on women's apparel appear in
the version of the *Blasme des fames* found in Ms.
671 of the Bibliothèque municipale in Rouen.
Similar lines are recorded in the versions of the
Blasme that belong to Family A (see Pfeffer essay).

Qui o fame prent compaignie
Oez si fet sens ou folie:
Fame si engigne e deçoit.
Celui que l'aime e qui la croit,
E fait son bon e son plaisir,   5
Ele se paine de lui traïr.
Tant com li hons li puet donner
Li fait ele semblant d'amer,
Mes quant el voit qu'il a petit,
Lors n'a cure de son delit.   10
Quant ele est richement peus
E de bele robe vestue,
Que la aumosniere de soie,
Chapeaus orfroie laz e coroie,
Fermauz d'argent e boen e leaus,   15
E les verge e les aneaus,
Trois ou quatre en chascune main,
Lors ne prise q'un poi le vilain
Qui gaigna a grant sueur
L'avoir done ele est a enneur.   20
Pour ce di ge foi que doi m'ame,
Mort est hon qui a male fame.

He who seeks female company
Hear if he acts with sense or folly:
Woman's trickster, a deceiver.
Those who love her and believe her,
Dote and cherish and obey,*   5
Those she'll be sure to betray.
As long as he has goods to share
Woman will pretend to care,
But when she finds his purse empty,
She tires of his company.   10
When she has richly dined
And dressed in robes so fine,
Silken purse hanging down,
Ribbons, belt, embroidered crown,*
Buckles of silver handsome and shining,   15
Golden rings and bangles binding,
Three or four upon each hand,
Then she cares little for the poor man
Who garnered by his sweating brow
The finery that bedecks her now.   20
Therefore say I, I swear on my life,
Doomed is he who has a bad wife.

Variants

Appendix

L = London; P = Paris 1593; Q = Paris 837; W = Westminster

Lines

1	*W:* Uns homs qui se marie
2	*LW:* Veiez si il fet sen ou folye; *P:* Ne fait pes sans ainz fait folie
3–5	*P: missing line*
6	*W:* Lors se pense de ly honnir
7	*W:* Tant fait elle semblant . . .
8–9	*W: missing lines*
10	*W:* . . . richement vestue
11	*W:* Si est alors le plus esmue
12	*P:* Que la aumosniere de soie; *W:* Quant elle a bourse et couroie
14	*PQW:* . . . bons et biaus
15	*W:* Et verges d'or et agneaulx
16	*W:* Quatre ou cinq en chacune main
20	*W:* Ce but elle a grant honnour
21	*W:* . . . foy que doy ma dame
22	*P:* . . . qui ai belle fame

Notes

Appendix

Lines

5   lit. "And does her will and her pleasure."
14 lit. "Hat embroidered with gold and silver thread, ribbons, and belt."

Selected Reading List

Baker, Derek, ed. *Medieval Women*. Oxford: Blackwell, 1978.

Ferrante, Joan M. *Woman as Image in Medieval Literature*. New York: Columbia University Press, 1975.

Gies, Frances, and Joseph Gies. *Marriage and the Family in the Middle Ages*. New York: Harper & Row, 1987.

Gold, Penny S. *The Lady and the Virgin: Image, Attitude, and Experience in Twelfth-Century France*. Chicago: University of Chicago Press, 1985.

Harksen, Sibylle. *Women in the Middle Ages*. Trans. Marianne Herzfeld. New York: Abner Schram, 1975.

Herlihy, David. *Women in Medieval Society*. The Smith History Lecture 1971. Houston, Tex.: The University of St. Thomas, 1971.

Labarge, Margaret Wade. *A Small Sound of the Trumpet: Women in Medieval Life*. Boston: Beacon Press, 1987.

Morewedge, R. T., ed. *The Role of Women in the Middle Ages*. Albany: State University of New York Press, 1975.

O'Faolain, Julia, and Lauro Martines, eds. *Not in God's Image*. New York: Harper & Row, 1973.

Shahar, Shulamith. *The Fourth Estate: A History of Women in the Middle Ages*. Trans. Chaya Galai. London: Methuen, 1983.

Stuard, Susan Mosher, ed. *Women in Medieval Society*. Philadelphia: University of Pennsylvania Press, 1976.

References

Aelianus, Claudius. 1958. *On the Characteristics of Animals*. Trans. A. F. Scholfield. Cambridge, Mass.: Harvard University Press.

"Amadas et Ydoine," roman du XIIIe siècle. 1926. Ed. John R. Reinhard. Classiques français du moyen âge 51. Paris: Honoré Champion.

Andreas Capellanus. 1941. *The Art of Courtly Love*. Ed. John Jay Parry. New York: Columbia University Press.

Aquinas, Thomas. 1947. *Summa Theologica*. Ed. and trans. the Fathers of the English Dominican Province. 3 vols. New York: Benzinger.

Aristotle. 1953. *Historia Animalium (On the Generation of Animals)*. Trans. A. L. Peck. Cambridge, Mass.: Harvard University Press.

Augustine. 1887. *De opere monachorum (On the Work of Monks)*. Trans. H. Browne. In vol. 3 of *A Select Library of Nicene Fathers*, ed. Philip Schaff. Buffalo: The Christian Literature Company.

Bell, Susan Groag. 1982. "Medieval Women Book Owners: Arbiters of Lay Piety and Ambassadors of Culture." *Signs* 7:742–68.

Berman, Constance H. 1985. "Women as Donors and Patrons to Southern French Monasteries in the Twelfth and Thirteenth Centuries." In *The Worlds of Medieval Women: Creativity, Influence, Imagination*, ed. Constance H. Berman, Charles W. Connell, Judith Rice Rothschild, 53–68. Morgantown: West Virginia University Press.

Bloch, Marc. 1966. *Feudal Society*. Trans. L. A. Manyon. Chicago: University of Chicago Press.

Bloch, R. Howard. 1977. *Medieval French Literature and Law*. Berkeley: University of California Press.

Boileau, Etienne. 1879. *Les Métiers et corporations de la ville de Paris, XIIIe siècle: Le Livre des métiers d'Etienne Boileau.* Ed. René de Lespinasse and François Bonnardot. Paris: Imprimerie nationale.

Bolton, Brenda M. 1976. "Mulieres sanctae." In *Women in Medieval Society,* ed. Susan Mosher Stuard, 141–65. Philadelphia: University of Pennsylvania Press.

Bornstein, Diane. 1983. *The Lady in the Tower: Medieval Courtesy Literature for Women.* Hamden, Conn.: Archon Books.

Brett, Edward Tracy. 1984. *Humbert of Romans: His Life and Views of Thirteenth-Century Society.* Studies and Texts 67. Toronto: Pontifical Institute of Mediaeval Studies.

Briquet, C. M. 1968. *Les Filigranes: Dictionnaire historique des marques du papier dès leur apparition vers 1282 jusqu'en 1600.* A facsimile of the 1907 edition. Ed. Allan Stevenson. Amsterdam: The Paper Publications Society.

Brissaud, Y. B. 1972. "L'Infanticide à la fin du moyen âge: Ses Motivations psychologiques et sa répression." *Revue historique du droit français et étranger* 50:229–56.

Bryant, Gwendolyn. 1984. "The French Heretic Beguine: Marguerite Porete." In *Medieval Women Writers,* ed. Katharina M. Wilson, 203–26. Athens: University of Georgia Press.

Bugge, John. 1975. *Virginitas: An Essay in the History of a Medieval Ideal.* International Archives of the History of Ideas, series minor 17. The Hague: Martinus Nijhoff.

Bullough, Vern L. 1973. "Medieval Medical and Scientific Views of Women." *Viator: Medieval and Renaissance Studies* 4:485–501.

Bullough, Vern L., and James Brundage. 1982. *Sexual Practices and the Medieval Church.* Buffalo, N.Y.: Prometheus Books.

Burgess, Glyn S. 1977. "Old French *Contenance* and *Contenant.*" In *Voices of Conscience: Essays on Medieval and Modern French Literature in Memory of James D. Powell and Rosemary Hodgins,* ed. Raymond J. Cormier, 21–41. Philadelphia: Temple University Press.

Bynum, Caroline Walker. 1982. *Jesus as Mother: Studies in the Spirituality of the High Middle Ages.* Berkeley: University of California Press.

Caird, G. B. 1971. "Paul and Women's Liberty." *Bulletin of the John Rylands Library* 54:268–81.

Casey, Kathleen. 1976. "The Cheshire Cat: Reconstructing the Experience of Medieval Women." In *Liberating Women's History,* ed. Bernice A. Carroll, 224–49. Urbana: University of Illinois Press.

Chaucer, Geoffrey. 1961. *The Canterbury Tales.* In *The Works of Geoffrey Chaucer,* ed. F. N. Robinson. 2d ed. Boston: Houghton Mifflin Co.

Chédeville, André, Jacques Le Goff, and Jacques Rossiaud. 1980. *La Ville médiévale.* Vol. 2 of *Histoire de la France urbaine.* Ed. Georges Duby. Paris: Seuil.

Chrétien de Troyes. 1959. *Le Roman de Perceval ou Le Conte du graal.* Ed. William Roach. Textes littéraires français 71. Geneva: Librairie Droz.

———. 1970. *Les Romans de Chrétien de Troyes, III. Le Chevalier de la charrete.* Ed. Mario Roques. Classiques français du moyen âge 86. Paris: Honoré Champion.

———. 1971. *Les Romans de Chrétien de Troyes, IV. Yvain.* Ed. Mario Roques. Classiques français du moyen âge 89. Paris: Honoré Champion.

Christine de Pizan. 1982. *The Book of the City of Ladies.* Trans. Earl Jeffrey Richards. New York: Persea Books.

Clement of Alexandria. 1954. *Christ the Educator.* Trans. Simon P. Wood. Vol. 23 of *The Fathers of the Church.* New York: Fathers of the Church.

Cooke, Thomas D. 1976. *The Old French and Chaucerian Fabliaux: A Study of Their Comic Climax.* Columbia: University of Missouri Press.

Cooke, Thomas D., and Benjamin Honeycutt, eds. 1974. *The Humor of the Fabliaux: A Collection of Critical Essays.* Columbia: University of Missouri Press.

Coulton, G. G. 1907. *From St. Francis to Dante: Translations from the Chronicle of the Franciscan Salimbene (1221–1288).* New York: Russell & Russell.

Cox, D. C., and Carter Revard. 1985. "A New ME O-and-I Lyric and Its Provenance." *Medium Aevum* 54:33–46.

Crane, Thomas Frederick, ed. 1890. *The "Exempla" or Illustrative Stories from the "Sermones Vulgares" of Jacques de Vitry.* London: Published for the Folklore Society by David Nutt.

Davis, Natalie Zemon. 1975. *Society and Culture in Early Modern France.* Stanford, Calif.: Stanford University Press.

d'Avray, David L., and M. Tausche. 1980. "Marriage Sermons in *ad status* Collections of the Central Middle Ages." *Archives d'histoire doctrinale et littéraire du moyen âge* 47: 71–119.

Donohue, Charles R. 1983. "Canon Law on the Formation of Marriage and Social Practice in the Later Middle Ages." *Journal of Family History* 8: 144–58.

Dronke, Peter. 1984. *Women Writers of the Middle Ages.* Cambridge: Cambridge University Press.

Duby, Georges. 1964. "Dans la France du Nord-Ouest au XIIe siècle: Les 'Jeunes' dans la société aristocratique." *Annales: Economies, sociétés, civilisations* 19:835–46.

————. 1977. *The Chivalrous Society.* Trans. Cynthia Postan. Berkeley: University of California Press.

————. 1978. *Medieval Marriage: Two Models from Twelfth-Century France.* Baltimore: Johns Hopkins Press, 1978.

Duplès-Agier, H. 1854. "Ordonnance somptuaire inédite de Philippe le Hardi." *Bibliothèque de l'Ecole des chartes* 15:176–81.

Erler, Mary, and Kowaleski, Maryanne, eds. 1988. *Women and Power in the Middle Ages.* Athens: University of Georgia Press.

Evans, Joan. 1952. *Dress in Medieval France.* Oxford: Clarendon Press.

Faral, Edmond. 1982. *Les Arts poétiques du XIIe et du XIIIe siècle: Recherches et documents sur la technique littéraire du moyen âge.* Paris: Champion, 1924. Reprint. Geneva: Slatkine.

Fawtier, Robert. 1962. *The Capetian Kings of France: Monarchy and Nation.* Trans. Lionel Butler and R. J. Adam. London: Macmillan & Co.

Ferrante, Joan M. 1975. *Woman as Image in Medieval Literature.* New York: Columbia University Press.

Foulet, Alfred, and Mary Blakely Speer. 1979. *On Editing Old French Texts.* Lawrence: Regents Press of Kansas.

Frederick II, Emperor of Germany. 1955. *The Art of Falconry: Being the De arte venandi cum avibus of Frederick II of Hohenstaufen.* Trans. and ed. C. A. Wood and F. M. Fyfe. London: Geoffrey Cumberledge.

Frey, Linda, Marsha Frey, and Joanne Schneider. 1982. *Women in Western European History.* Westport, Conn.: Greenwood Press.

Friedmann, Herbert. 1980. *A Bestiary for Saint Jerome.* Washington, D. C.: Smithsonian Institution Press.

Gaston Phébus. 1971. *Livre de chasse.* Ed. Gunnar Tilander. Karlshamn: E. G. Johannsons.

Geoffrey of Vinsauf. 1967. *Poetria Nova of Geoffrey of Vinsauf.* Trans. Margaret F. Nims. Toronto: Pontifical Institute of Mediaeval Studies.

Gies, Frances, and Joseph Gies. 1978. *Women in the Middle Ages.* New York: Thomas Y. Crowell Co.

———. 1987. *Marriage and the Family in the Middle Ages.* New York: Harper & Row, 1987.

Glinsky, Jerzy, ed. 1971. *Proverbs.* Amsterdam: Elsevier Publishing Co.

Godefroy, F. 1938. *Dictionnaire de l'ancienne langue française.* 10 vols. Paris: Librairie des sciences et des arts.

Gold, Penny S. 1985. *The Lady and the Virgin: Image, Attitude, and Experience in Twelfth-Century France.* Chicago: University of Chicago Press.

Gosman, Martin, ed. 1982. *La Lettre du Prêtre Jean.* Mediaevalia Groningana 2. Groningen: Bouma's Boekhuis bv.

Greenfield, Kent R. 1918. *Sumptuary Law in Nürnberg: A Study in Paternal Government.* Johns Hopkins University Studies in Historical and Political Science, series 36, no. 2. Baltimore: Johns Hopkins Press.

Grundriss der romanischen Literaturen des Mittelalters. 1970. Vol. 6: *La Littérature didactique, allégorique et satirique.* Ed. Hans-Robert Jauss. Vol. 2. Heidelberg: Carl Winter.

Guillaume de Lorris, and Jean de Meun. 1970–73. *Le Roman de la Rose,* vols. 2, 3, ed. Félix Lecoy. Classiques français du moyen âge 95, 98. Paris: Honoré Champion.

Guillaume le Clerc. 1936. *The Bestiary of Guillaume le Clerc.* Trans. George C. Druce. Ashford, Kent: Headly Brothers.

Hadju, Robert. 1980. "The Position of Noblewomen in the *pays de coutumes,* 1100–1300." *Journal of Family History* 5: 122–44.

Hallam, Elizabeth M. 1980. *Capetian France, 987–1328.* London: Longman.

Hanawalt, Barbara A. 1976. "The Female Felon in Fourteenth-Century England." In *Women in Medieval Society,* ed. Susan Mosher Stuard, 125–40. Philadelphia: University of Pennsylvania Press.

———. 1986. *The Ties That Bound: Peasant Families in Medieval England.* New York: Oxford University Press.

Herlihy, David. 1984. "Demography." In *Dictionary of the Middle Ages,* ed. Joseph R. Strayer, 4:136–48. New York: Charles Scribner's Sons.

———. 1985. *Medieval Households.* Cambridge, Mass.: Harvard University Press.

Heyse, Paul. 1856. *Romanische Inedita auf italiänischen Bibliotheken.* Berlin: Wilhelm Hertz.

Holzknecht, K. J. 1966. *Literary Patronage in the Middle Ages.* New York: Octagon Books.

Horowitz, Maryanne Cline. 1976. "Aristotle and Woman." *Journal of the History of Biology* 9:183–213.

Houston, Mary. 1979. *Medieval Costume in England and France: The Thirteenth, Fourteenth and Fifteenth Centuries.* London: Adam Charles Black.

Howell, Martha, C. 1986. *Women, Production, and Patriarchy in Late Medieval Cities.* Chicago: University of Chicago Press.

Hughes, Muriel J. 1943. *Women Healers in Medieval Life and Literature.* New York: King's Crown Press.

Institut de recherche et d'histoire des texts, section romane. N.d. "Notice du manuscrit Florence laurentienne Pluteus 41, 42." Paris: IRHT.

Isidoro de Sevilla. 1951. *Etimologías.* Madrid: Biblioteca de Auctores Christianos.

Jacquart, D. 1981. *Le Milieu médical en France du XIIe au XIVe siècle.* Hautes Etudes médiévales et modernes 46 du Centre de recherches d'histoire et de philologie V. Geneva: Librairie Droz.

Jarrett, Bede. 1926. *Social Theories of the Middle Ages, 1200–1500.* London: Ernest Benn.

Jodogne, Omer. 1959. "L'Édition de l'*Evangile aux femmes.*" In *Studi in onore di Angelo Monteverdi,* 1:353–75. Modena: Società tipografica editrice modenese.

Jubinal, Achille, ed. 1835. *Jongleurs et trouvères ou Choix de saluts: Épitres, rêveries et autres pièces légères des XIIIe et XIVe siècles.* Paris: Merklein.

————, ed. 1842. *Nouveau Recueil de contes, dits, fabliaux et autres pièces inédites des XIIIe, XIVe, et XVe siècles.* Paris: Challamel.

Katzenellenbogen, Adolf. 1959. *The Sculptural Programs of Chartres Cathedral.* New York: W. W. Norton.

Kellum, Barbara A. 1974. "Infanticide in England in the Later Middle Ages." *History of Childhood Quarterly* 1:367–88.

Kennedy, Thomas Corbin. 1973. "Anglo-Norman Poems about Love, Women, and Sex from British Museum MS. Harley 2253." Ph.D. diss. Columbia University.

Ker, N. R. 1965. *Facsimile of British Museum MS. Harley 2253.* Early English Text Society 255. London: Oxford University Press.

Kirschner, Julius. 1985. "Wives' Claims against Insolvent Husbands in Late Medieval Italy." In *Women of the Medieval World,* ed. Julius Kirshner and Suzanne F. Wemple, 256–303. New York: Basil Blackwell.

Klingender, Francis. 1971. *Animals in Art and Thought to the End of the Middle Ages.* Cambridge, Mass.: The MIT Press.

Kraemer, Pierre. 1920. *Le Luxe et les lois somptuaires au moyen âge.* Paris: E. Sagot.

Kraus, Henry. 1982. "Eve and Mary: Conflicting Images of Medieval Woman." In *Feminism and Art History: Questioning the Litany,* ed. Norma Broude and Mary D. Garrard, 79–99. New York: Harper & Row.

Labarge, Margaret Wade. 1987. *A Small Sound of the Trumpet: Women in Medieval Life.* Boston: Beacon Press.

Långfors, Arthur. 1916. *Notice du manuscrit français 12483 de la Bibliothèque nationale.* Paris: Imprimerie nationale.

————. 1918. "La Société française vers 1330, vue par un frère prêcheur du soissonnais." *Öfversigt af Finska Vetenskaps-Societetens För-*

handlingar. Bx LX (1917–18), 1–23. Afd. B. No. 1. Helsinki: Helsingfors Centraltryckeri.

———. 1970. *Les Incipit des poèmes français antérieurs au 16e siècle: Répertoire bibliographique.* 1917. Reprint. New York: Burt Franklin.

Langlois, Charles V. 1969. *Saint Louis—Philippe le Bel: Les Derniers Capétiens directs (1226–1328).* Vol. 3, part 2 of *Histoire de France depuis les origines jusqu'à la révolution.* Ed. Ernest Lavisse. 1900–11. Reprint. New York: AMS Press.

Langlois, Ernest. 1899. "Anciens Proverbes français." *Bibliothèque de l'Ecole des chartes* 60:569–601.

La Tour Landry, Geoffrey de. N.d. *The Book of the Knight of La Tour-Landry,* ed. G. S. Taylor. London: John Hamilton.

Legge, M. Dominica. 1950. *Anglo-Norman in the Cloisters.* Edinburgh: University Press.

Lehmann, Andrée. 1952. *Le Rôle de la femme dans l'histoire de France au moyen âge.* Paris: Berger-Levrault.

Lemay, Helen. 1978. "Some Thirteenth- and Fourteenth-Century Lectures on Female Sexuality." *International Journal of Women's Studies* 1:391–400.

———. 1985. "Anthonius Guainerius and Medieval Gynecology." In *Women of the Medieval World,* ed. Julius Kirshner and Suzanne F. Wemple, 317–36. New York: Basil Blackwell.

Livingston, Charles H. 1951. *Le Jongleur Gautier le Leu: Etude sur les fabliaux.* Cambridge, Mass.: Harvard University Press.

Lucas, Angela M. 1983. *Women in the Middle Ages: Religion, Marriage, and Letters.* New York: St. Martin's Press.

McCash, June Hall. In press. "Women as Patrons of Medieval Literature." In *Encyclopedia of Medieval Women Writers,* ed. Katharina M. Wilson. Athens: University of Georgia.

McCulloch, Francis. 1962. *Medieval Latin and French Bestiaries.* University of North Carolina Studies in Romance Languages and Literatures 33. Chapel Hill: University of North Carolina Press.

McLaughlin, Eleanor. 1974. "Equality of Souls, Inequality of Sexes:

Women in Medieval Theology." In *Religion and Sexism: Images of Women in the Jewish and Christian Tradition,* ed. Rosemary Ruether, 213–66. New York: Simon & Schuster.

———. 1980. "Women, Power, and the Pursuit of Holiness in Medieval Christianity." In *Women of Spirit. Female Leadership in the Jewish and Christian Traditions,* ed. Rosemary Ruether and Eleanor McLaughlin, 99–130. New York: Simon & Schuster.

McNamara, JoAnn. 1983. *A New Song: Celibate Women in the First Three Christian Centuries.* New York: Haworth Press.

McNamara, JoAnn, and Suzanne F. Wemple. 1977. "Sanctity and Power: The Dual Pursuit of Medieval Women." In *Becoming Visible: Women in European History,* ed. Renate Bridenthal and Claudia Koonz, 90–118. Boston: Houghton Mifflin Co.

McNeill, John T., and H. M. Gamer. 1971. *Medieval Handbooks of Penance.* New York: Columbia University Press.

Mâle, Emile 1958. *Religious Art in France in the Thirteenth Century.* Trans. D. Nussy. New York: Harper & Row.

Maloux, Maurice. 1980. *Dictionnaire des proverbes, sentences et maximes.* Paris: Larousse.

Maranda, Pierre. 1974. *French Kinship Structure and History.* Janua Linguarum, Series Practica 169. The Hague: Mouton.

Markun, Leo. 1926. *Prostitution in the Medieval World.* Giraud, Kans.: Haldemon-Julius Co.

Marrow, James. 1977. "*Circumdederunt me canes multi:* Christ's Tormentors in Northern European Art of the Late Middle Ages and Renaissance." *Art Bulletin* 59:167–81.

Matheolus. 1892–1905. *Les Lamentations de Matheolus et le Livre de leesce de Jehan le Fèvre, de Resson (poèmes français du XIVe siècle).* Ed. A.-G. van Hamel. Bibliothèque de l'Ecole des hautes études 95–96. Paris: Emile Bouillon.

Matthew of Vendôme. 1981. *Ars Versificatoria (The Art of the Versemaker).* Trans. Roger P. Parr. Mediaeval Philosophical Texts in Translation 22. Milwaukee, Wis.: Marquette University Press.

Meier-Ewert, Charity N. 1970–71. "A Study and a Partial Edition of the Anglo-Norman Verse in the Bodleian Manuscript Digby 86." D.Phil. Oxford.

Ménard, Philippe. 1983. *Les Fabliaux: Contes à rire du moyen âge*. Paris: Presses universitaires de France.

Merrilees, Brian S. 1971. "'Il n'i a lange ke put parler . . .': Words against Women." *Medium Aevum* 40:6–9.

Meyer, Paul. 1872. "Henri d'Andeli et le Chancelier Philippe." *Romania* 1:190–215.

———. 1875. "Notice d'un recueil manuscrit de poésies françaises du XIIIe au XVe siècle, appartenant à Westminster Abbey." *Bulletin de la Société des anciens textes français* 1:25–36.

———. 1877. "Mélanges de poésie française, IV: Plaidoyer en faveur des femmes." *Romania* 6:499–503.

———. 1883. "Notice du MS A. 454 de la Bibliothèque de Rouen." *Bulletin de la Société des anciens textes français* 9:76–111.

———. 1886. "Les Manuscrits français de Cambridge, II: Bibliothèque de l'Université." *Romania* 15:236–357.

Mihm, Madelyn Timmel, ed. 1984. *The Songe d'Enfer of Raoul de Houdenc: An Edition Based on All the Extant Manuscripts*. Beihefte zur Zeitschrift für romanische Philologie 190. Tübingen: Max Niemeyer.

Miller, B. D. H. 1963. "The Early History of Bodleian MS. Digby 86." *Duquesne Studies: Annuale Medievale* 4:23–56.

Montaiglon, Anatole de, and Gaston Raynaud. N.d. *Recueil général et complet des fabliaux des XIIIe et XIVe siècles*. 6 vols. 1872. Reprint. New York: Burt Franklin.

Morawski, Joseph, ed. 1925. *Proverbes français antérieurs au XVe siècle*. Classiques français du moyen âge 47. Paris: Honoré Champion.

Morris, Richard, ed. 1973. *Old English Homilies and Homiletic Treatises of the Twelfth and Thirteenth Centuries*. Edited from MSS in the British Museum, Lambeth and Bodleian Libraries. Early English Text Society, o.s. nos. 29 and 34, 1869. Reprint. New York: Kraus.

Mundy, John Hines. 1982. "Urban Society and Culture: Toulouse and Its

Region." In *Renaissance and Renewal in the Twelfth Century,* ed. Robert L. Benson and Giles Constable, 229–47. Cambridge, Mass.: Harvard University Press.

Mundy, John Hines, and Peter Riesenberg. 1958. *The Medieval Town.* New York: Van Nostrand Reinhold Co.

Muscatine, Charles. 1986. *The Old French Fabliaux.* New Haven: Yale University Press.

Newhall, Richard A., ed. 1953. *The Chronicle of Jean de Venette.* Trans. Jean Birdsall. New York: Columbia University Press.

Noonan, John T., Jr. 1973. "Power to Choose." *Viator: Medieval and Renaissance Studies* 4:419–34.

Nykrog, Per. 1957. *Les Fabliaux: Etude d'histoire littéraire et de stylistique médiévale.* Copenhagen: Ejnar Munksgaard.

O'Faolain, Julia, and Lauro Martines, eds. 1973. *Not in God's Image.* New York: Harper & Row.

Omont, Henri. 1905. "Notice sur quelques feuillets retrouvés d'un manuscrit français de la Bibliothèque de Dijon." *Romania* 34:364–74.

———. 1932. *Fabliaux et contes en vers français du XIIIe siècle: facsimilé du manuscrit français 837 de la Bibliothèque nationale.* Paris: Ernest Leroux.

Otis, Leah L. 1985. *Prostitution in Medieval Society.* Chicago: University of Chicago Press.

Oulmont, Charles. 1972. *Les Débats du clerc et du chevalier dans la littérature poétique du moyen âge.* Paris: 1911. Reprint. Geneva: Slatkine.

The Owl and the Nightingale. 1960. Ed. Eric Gerald Stanley. Nelson's Medieval and Renaissance Library. London: Thomas Nelson and Sons.

Paris, Gaston. 1875. "Notice du manuscrit de la Bibliothèque de Dijon N° 298²." *Bulletin de la Société des anciens textes français* 1:44–49.

———. 1971. "Dits." In vol. 23 of *Histoire littéraire de la France,* 266–86. Paris, 1856. Reprint. Nendeln, Liechtenstein: Kraus.

Parkes, M. J. 1969. *English Cursive Bookhands, 1250–1500.* Oxford: Clarendon Press.

Parmisano, Fabian. 1969. "Love and Marriage in the Middle Ages." *New Blackfriars* 50:599–608, 649–60.

Parvey, Constance F. 1974. "The Theology and Leadership of Women in the New Testament." In *Religion and Sexism: Images of Women in Jewish and Christian Tradition,* ed. Rosemary Ruether, 117–49. New York: Simon & Schuster.

Patch, H. R. 1950. *The Other World According to Descriptions in Medieval Literature.* Cambridge, Mass.: Harvard University Press.

Payen, Jean-Charles. 1977. "La Crise du mariage à la fin du XIIIe siècle d'après la littérature française du temps." In *Famille et parenté dans l'occident médiéval: Actes du colloque de Paris (6–8 juin 1974),* ed. Georges Duby and Jacques Le Goff, 413–26. Rome: Ecole française de Rome, Palais Farnese.

Pegues, Franklin J. 1962. *The Lawyers of the Last Capetians.* Princeton, N.J.: Princeton University Press.

Petroff, Elizabeth A. 1986. *Medieval Women's Visionary Literature.* New York: Oxford University Press.

Physiologus. 1979. Trans. Michael J. Curley. Austin: University of Texas Press.

Pike, Joseph B. 1938. *Frivolities of Courtiers and Footprints of Philosophers. Being a Translation of the First, Second, and Third Books and Selections from the Seventh and Eighth Books of the "Policraticus" of John of Salisbury.* Minneapolis: University of Minnesota Press.

Pineaux, Jacques. 1979. *Proverbes et dictons français.* Que sais-je 706. 7th ed. Paris: Presses universitaires de France.

Piponnier, François. 1970. *Costume et vie sociale: La Cour d'Anjou, XIVe–XVe siècles.* Paris: Mouton.

Plummer, John F., ed. 1982. *Vox Feminae: Studies in Medieval Woman's Songs.* Studies in Medieval Culture 15. Kalamazoo, Mich.: Medieval Institute Publications.

Pope, M. K. 1954. *From Latin to Modern French with Especial Consideration of Anglo-Norman: Phonology and Morphology.* 1934. Reprint. Manchester, Eng.: Manchester University Press.

Power, Eileen. 1975. *Medieval Women.* Ed. M. M. Postan. Cambridge: Cambridge University Press.

Purtle, Carol. 1982. *The Marian Paintings of Jan van Eyck.* Princeton: Princeton University Press.

Raynaud de Lage, Guy. 1981. *Introduction à l'ancien français.* Paris: SEDES.

Revard, Carter. 1979. "Richard Hurd and Ms. Harley 2253." *Notes and Queries* 224 (n.s. 26): 199–202.

———. 1982. "Gilote et Johane: An Interlude in B.L. MS. Harley 2253." *Studies in Philology* 71:122–46.

———. 1988. Letter to Wendy Pfeffer, 1 January.

Rezak, Brigitte Bedos. 1985. "An Image from a Medieval Woman's World: The Seal of Jeanne de Châtillon, Countess of Alençon, 1271." In *The Worlds of Medieval Women: Creativity, Influence, Imagination,* ed. Constance H. Berman, Charles W. Connell, Judith Rice Rothschild, xi–xiii. Morgantown: West Virginia University Press.

Rigg, A. G., ed. 1986. *Gawain on Marriage: The Textual Tradition of the "De Coniuge Non Ducenda" with Critical Edition and Translation.* Studies and Texts 79. Toronto: Pontifical Institute of Mediaeval Studies.

Roberts, Phyllis B. 1985. "Stephen Langton's *Sermo de Virginibus.*" In *Women of the Medieval World: Essays in Honor of John H. Mundy,* ed. Julius Kirshner and Suzanne F. Wemple, 103–18. Oxford: Basil Blackwell.

Rokseth, Yvonne. 1935. "Les Femmes musiciennes du XIIe au XIVe siècle." *Romania* 61:464–80.

Rossiaud, Jacques. 1988. *Medieval Prostitution.* Trans. Ludia G. Cochrane. New York: Blackwell.

Rowland, Beryl. 1973. *Animals with Human Faces: A Guide to Animal Symbolism.* Knoxville: University of Tennessee Press.

———. 1977. *Birds with Human Souls: A Guide to Bird Symbolism.* Knoxville: University of Tennessee Press.

Ruether, Rosemary R. 1977. *Mary: The Feminine Face of the Church.* Philadelphia: Westminster Press.

———. 1979. "Misogynism and Virginal Feminism in the Fathers of the Church." In *Women in Western Thought,* ed. Martha Lee Osborne, 62–65. New York: Random House.

Sachs, Curt. 1955. *Our Musical Heritage: A Short History of Music.* Englewood Cliffs, N.J.: Prentice-Hall.

Schalk, Fritz. 1968. "Die moralische und literarische Satire." Vol. 2:

"Contes, Dits and Fabliaux," In *Grundriss der romanischen Literaturen des Mittelalters*. Vol. 6: *La Littérature didactique, allégorique et satirique*. Ed. Hans-Robert Jauss, 1:249–53. Heidelberg: Carl Winter.

Schultz-Busacker, Elisabeth. 1985. *Proverbes et expressions proverbiales dans la littérature narrative du moyen âge français: Recueil et analyse*. Paris: Honoré Champion.

Scott, Margaret. 1980. *Late Gothic Europe, 1400–1500*. The History of Dress Series, ed. Aileen Ribeiro. Atlantic Highlands, N.J.: Humanities Press.

Shahar, Shulamith. 1983. *The Fourth Estate: A History of Women in the Middle Ages*. Trans. Chaya Galai. London: Methuen.

Singer, Samuel. 1944–47. *Sprichwörter des Mittelalters*. 3 vols. Bern, Switz.: Peter Lang.

Sronkova, Olga. 1954. *Gothic Women's Fashion*. Trans. Greta Hort. Prague: Artia.

Stengel, E. 1871. *Codicem Manu Scriptum Digby 86 in bibliotheca Bodleiana Asservatum*. Halle, Germ.: Libraria Orphanotrophei.

Stiennon, Jacques, and Geneviève Hasenohr. 1982. *La Paléographie du moyen âge*. 1973. Reprint. Paris: Collection Universitaire.

Strayer, Joseph R. 1971. "The Development of Feudal Institutions." In *Medieval Statecraft and the Perspectives of History*, 77–89. Princeton, N.J.: Princeton University Press.

———. 1980. *The Reign of Philip the Fair*. Princeton, N.J.: Princeton University Press.

Tertullian. 1959. "The Apparel of Women." Trans. Edwin A. Quain. In *Disciplinary, Moral and Ascetical Works*, trans. Rudolph Arbesmann, Emily Scoter, Joseph Daly, and Edwin A. Quain, 117–49. Vol. 40 of *The Fathers of the Church*. New York: Fathers of the Church.

Thrupp, Sylvia L., ed. 1964. *Change in Medieval Society: Europe North of the Alps, 1050–1500*. New York: Appleton-Century-Crofts.

Verdier, Philippe. 1980. *Le Couronnement de la Vierge: Les Origines et les premiers développements d'un thème iconographique*. Conférence Albert le Grand, 1972. Montréal, Institut d'études médiévales. Paris: J. Vrin.

Vincent, John Martin. 1935. *Costume and Conduct in the Laws of Basel, Bern, and Zurich*. Baltimore: Johns Hopkins Press.

Vising, Johan. 1970. *Anglo-Norman Language and Literature*. London: Oxford University Press, 1923. Reprint. Westport, Conn.: Greenwood Press.

Walther, Hans. 1959–69. *Carmina Medii Aevi Posterioris Latina. I. Initia Carminum ac Versuum medii aevi posterioris latinorum*. Göttingen: Vandenhoeck & Ruprecht.

————. 1966. *Proverbia sententiaeque Latinitatis Medii Aevi = Lateinische Sprichwörter und Sentenzen des Mittelalters*. 5 vols. Göttingen: Vandenhoeck & Ruprecht.

Warner, Marina. 1976. *Alone of All Her Sex: The Myth and the Cult of the Virgin Mary*. New York: Alfred A. Knopf.

Wemple, Suzanne Fonay. 1981. *Women in Frankish Society: Marriage and the Cloister, 500 to 900*. Philadelphia: University of Pennsylvania Press.

Wessley, Stephen E. 1978. "The Guglielmites: Salvation through Women." In *Medieval Women*, ed. Derek Baker, 289–303. Oxford: Blackwell.

White, T. H., trans. 1954. *The Bestiary, a Book of Beasts*. New York: G. P. Putnam's Sons.

Wright, Thomas, and James Orchard Halliwell, eds. 1841–43. *Reliquiae Antiquae: Scraps from Ancient Manuscripts Illustrating Chiefly Early English Literature and the English Language*. 2 vols. London: William Pickering.

Yver, Jean. 1966. *Egalité entre héritiers et exclusion des enfants dotés*. Paris: Sirey.

Zumthor, Paul. 1972. *Essai de poétique médiévale*. Paris: Seuil.

Index